Nonprint Production for Students, Teachers, and Media Specialists

Nonprint Production
for
Students, Teachers, and
Media Specialists

A Step-by-Step Guide

Second Edition

James L. Thomas

1988
LIBRARIES UNLIMITED, INC.
Englewood, Colorado

LIBRARIES UNLIMITED, INC.
P.O. Box 3988
Englewood, Colorado 80155-3988

Library of Congress Cataloging-in-Publication Data

Thomas, James L., 1945-
    Nonprint production for students, teachers, and media specialists.

    Bibliography: p. 133
    Includes index.
    1. Teaching--Aids and devices.   2. Audio-visual materials.   I. Title.
LB1043.T487   1988   371.3'3   88-26727
ISBN 0-87287-591-1

This book is bound with Type II nonwoven material that meets and exceeds National Association of State Textbook Administrators' Type II nonwoven material specifications Class A through E.

Contents

Preface ix

Acknowledgments xi

Introduction xiii

1—STORYBOARDING AND SCRIPTING........................1
   Introduction 1
   Objective 2
   Strategies 2
   Definition of Terms...2
   Materials and Costs...2
   Procedure for Production....................................3
   Sample Format for Storyboarding 10
   Suggestions for Follow-up Activities.........................16
   Tapping Local Resources....................................16
   Sources for Equipment and Supplies.........................17
   Annotated Bibliography.....................................18

2 – COMPUTER GRAPHICS............................19
Introduction 19
Objective 21
Strategies 22
Definition of Terms..................................23
Materials and Costs..................................24
Operation Checklist for Computer Graphics Program...........25
Procedure for Production.............................26
Sample Format.......................................27
Outline for Using Computer Graphics Program.................28
Suppliers of Hardware and Software...................29
Selected Computer Software Review Sources.................31
Suggestions for Follow-up Activities.........................32
Tapping Local Resources..............................33
Annotated Bibliography...............................33

3 – TRANSPARENCY LIFTS AND LAMINATION...............36
Introduction 36
Objectives 36
Strategies 37
Definition of Terms..................................37
Materials and Costs..................................40
Operation Checklist for the Dry Mount Press.................42
Operation Checklist for the Overhead Projector...............43
Procedure for Production.............................43
Sample Format.......................................56
Suggestions for Follow-up Activities.........................59
Tapping Local Resources..............................61
Sources of Equipment and Supplies...................61
Annotated Bibliography...............................62

4 – SLIDE/TAPE AND FILMSTRIP/TAPE
PRESENTATIONS 65
Introduction 65
Definition of Terms..................................65

Materials and Costs..68
   Equipment...68
      Camera...68
      Close-up rings.....................................68
      Copy stand...68
      Cable release......................................69
      Tripod 69
      Light box or slide sorter..........................69
      Slide projector....................................69
      Sound slide projectors with built-in screen........69
      Filmstrip projector and/or viewer..................70
      Cassette tape recorder.............................70
   Supplies 70
      Cassette tapes.....................................70
      Film 70
      Processing 71
Operation Checklist for the 35mm SLR Camera.................72
Operation Checklist for the Slide Projector.................74
Operation Checklist for the Filmstrip Projector.............75
Operation Checklist for the Cassette Audiotape Recorder.....76
Basic Considerations..77
   Art Work..77
   Format of the Pictures..................................77
   Content of the Pictures.................................77
   Size of the Pictures....................................78
   Helpful Hints...78
   Film for the 35mm Camera: Choice and Loading............78
   Taping the Narration....................................80
Sources for Equipment and Supplies..........................80
Slide/Tape Presentations—Overview...........................82
Objectives 82
Strategies 82
Procedure for Production....................................83
   The 35mm Camera: Copy Stand or Tripod...................83
   Camera on Copy Stand....................................84
   Camera on a Tripod......................................85
   Placement of Slides in the Projector....................86
   The Showing...86
   Making a Copy of the Tape and Slides....................86
Sample Format and Evaluation for Making a
Slide/Tape Presentation.....................................87
Suggestions for Follow-up Activities........................90
Tapping Local Resources.....................................93
Filmstrip/Tape Presentations—Overview.......................93

**4 — SLIDE/TAPE AND FILMSTRIP/TAPE
PRESENTATIONS — *Continued***
Objectives 94
Strategies 94
Procedure for Production....................................95
   Placement of Pictures for Photographing..................95
   Camera on Copy Stand....................................96
   Camera on Tripod..98
   Taping the Narration....................................99
   Copying the Filmstrip/Tape Presentation..................99
Sample Format and Evaluation for Making a Filmstrip.........100
Suggestions for Follow-up Activities.........................102
Tapping Local Resources....................................105
Annotated Bibliography....................................106
   Slide/Tape Presentations...............................106
   Filmstrips..110

5 — SINGLE-CAMERA TELEVISION PROGRAMS..............112
Introduction 112
Objective 113
Strategies 113
Definition of Terms..114
Materials and Costs..115
Operation Checklist for the Video System.....................116
Procedure for Production...................................118
Sample Format...120
Suggestions for Follow-up Activities.........................124
Tapping Local Resources...................................125
Sources for Equipment and Supplies.........................126
Annotated Bibliography....................................127

Sources of Additional Information.........................133

Index 139

Preface

As audiovisual equipment changes and new items emerge, techniques for production and use of equipment and materials need to be examined. A revision of *Nonprint Production for Students, Teachers, and Media Specialists* has been published to reflect these advancements.

A variety of reasons may be put forth for offering this updated resource. Newly published reference manuals and textbooks reflect the continued growth and interest in the topic. Practicing teachers and librarians have brought to the author's attention new developments in equipment and production techniques. And finally, knowledge of these techniques for local production of instructional materials and operation of equipment in the schools obviously remains necessary for most teachers and librarians.

Three noticeable differences have occurred between the first and second editions; namely, a new chapter has been added, one has been deleted, and two have been combined. Elements of graphic design and computer-generated materials are of major importance to teachers and students in the school setting. The chapter on this comes immediately after storyboarding and scripting, since much of what is discussed and displayed could be used in the nonprint production chapters. The chapter on super 8mm productions was deleted; few schools now have the equipment necessary to carry out the procedures. And finally, slide/tape and filmstrip/tape presentations were combined with a discussion of basic considerations dealing with art work, composition of the picture, elements of photography, etc., first, followed with the unique steps for making slides and filmstrips.

Of concern to a few readers has been this author's resistance to label the activities discussed "for younger children" or "for older students." The user will still not find such labeling in this edition. It is my feeling that all the techniques in this book may be attempted, IF explained by a teacher in advance, with students in grades one through twelve without difficulty. Using adult judgment in a learning or instructional situation should be the key to appropriateness for a certain age group.

In comparing this edition with the previous one, the user will note that each chapter has been checked for accuracy and currency of information. As equipment and software have changed over the past few years, these changes have been noted and updated. At the end of each chapter the user will find a revised bibliography which includes articles, monographs, reference books, directories, and nonprint items dealing with the topics discussed.

As in the past, constructive criticism and advice is encouraged. Suggestions for improvement or additions for future editions through correspondence via the publisher to the author will be most helpful and appreciated.

James L. Thomas
Associate Professor
School of Library and
Information Studies
Texas Woman's University

Acknowledgments

The author wishes to thank a number of individuals who made this edition possible. First, my typist, Lorrie Fiel, who put up with my constant need for revisions. Second, the staff of the University library, especially Rita Yribar and Margaret MacDougall. Third, John Bennett and Debbie Fowlston, who did the difficult task of locating information for the bibliography and proofed the finished copy. And finally, my boss, Brooke Sheldon, who always had words of encouragement along with plenty of smiles.

Introduction

Why is an author motivated to write a book on nonprint production? In recent years, reports in all areas of education have revealed a continuing interest in and demand for increasing the skills of students, teachers, and media specialists in the production of nonprint materials. Sample statements from nine different educators attest to the value to be realized from such activity:

> My experiences with children in media-related learning activities lead to one conclusion: media are tools for children. Using media gives them a chance to say who they are, where they are, how they think and how they see the world.[1]

> From encouraging children to produce audiovisual materials, it is possible that teachers will be able to discern, through observation of what a student chooses, which of the learning modes is best suited for the individual child. We talk a good deal about providing the best materials for each child's learning style, but not much is done about it. If this could be done, how much more motivated the pupils would be, for their individualism would be recognized.[2]

> Student productions can play a significant role in the classroom learning experience. The benefits to the producers are certainly manifold. In addition, the majority of student users react very positively to judicious use of the productions.[3]

> If students discover that they can improve their reading, even slightly, through participation in media productions, they may feel even more motivated to read in other instances. If students experience some success in an academic area that was previously frustrating and discouraging, they are likely to feel an increase in self-esteem. This increase often translates into greater efforts in the classroom, both academically and socially.[4]

> By putting media materials in the hands of children, educators can capitalize on the inherent intellectual curiosity and learning potential each child is born with. Media allows the child to explore the external world and himself, and exploration is fundamental to the learning process.[5]

> When students work together to successfully plan and produce a ... [nonprint production] ... of a school or community activity, they take part in a mentally vigorous process. For students of any age, such an activity can be a stimulus to growth and toward visual intelligence, which means toward better interpretation and understanding of meanings and expressions that take visual forms and require visual decisions in their lives.[6]

John Culkin further explains in his chapter "Education in a Post-Literate World" that elementary and secondary students desperately need to be involved in their own educational process: to be active, independent learners instead of passive, dependent recipients of instruction. "The learner these days comes to school with a vast reservoir of vicarious experiences ...; he wants to be involved in what he is doing; he wants to use all his senses in his learning as an active agent in the process of discovery."[7]

This book is intended to be a step-by-step manual that offers the beginner information on nonprint production of materials through a nonthreatening instructional format. Each chapter is systematically arranged for easy reading so that, at a glance, the reader can determine (1) the specific objective(s) of the process, (2) the strategies to be used in winning over a group, (3) the definition of any terms that might be unfamiliar to the reader, (4) the materials to be used and the maximum costs expected, (5) checklists containing the steps to be taken in operating each piece of equipment to be used in the production and/or presentation, (6) the exact step-by-step procedure to use in producing the item, (7) a sample format from an actual graphic produced by students, (8) suggested follow-up activities, (9) ideas for using local resource people, (10) a list of possible suppliers of the equipment and software items used in each production, and (11) an annotated bibliography.

Since the first and second editions of the book, the author has interacted with graduate students in librarianship and education, practitioners, and young people in an effort to refine the original text. Also, particular attention has been paid to the comments shared by the reviewers. The author contends, therefore, that this text is an improvement in arrangement, representing an update of prices and new developments in nonprint technology.

For those individuals desiring supportive documentation on the ways nonprint has been used across the school curriculum, the author has compiled two readings for reference, also published by Libraries Unlimited: *Nonprint in the Elementary Curriculum* (1982; out of print) and *Nonprint in the Secondary Curriculum* (1982). Either or both of these books would be beneficial for discovering how practitioners have used nonprint in innovative ways in particular subject areas.

In conclusion, the author encourages reactions to this volume. Only through constructive criticism can a text such as this change and specific needs be met. If students, teachers, and media specialists are willing to share their successes and failures as they experience and experiment with nonprint productions, future editions will reflect this input.

NOTES

[1]Julius F. Schillinger, "Media Are Tools for Children," *Audiovisual Instruction* 21 (March 1976): 67.

[2]Carol Carlisle, "For Reluctance: Media Production Motivation," *Audiovisual Instruction* 19 (March 1974): 7.

[3]Roy Ferguson and Jon Shorr, "Seeing Is Believing: Visual Communication and the Social Studies," *Social Education* 40 (May 1976): 279.

[4]David Barber-Smith and Susan S. Reilly, "Use Media to Motivate Reading," *Audiovisual Instruction* 22 (December 1977): 34.

[5]Schillinger, "Media Are Tools," 69.

[6]Jerrold E. Kemp and Deane K. Dayton, *Planning and Producing Instructional Media*, 5th ed. (New York: Harper & Row, 1985): 9.

[7]John Culkin, "Education in a Post-Literate World," in *The Mediate Teacher: Seminal Essays on Creative Teaching*, selected and introduced by Frank McLaughlin (Philadelphia: North American Publishing Co., 1975), 17.

1

Storyboarding and Scripting

INTRODUCTION

Anyone who has taught knows that an instructional lesson does not have an obscure beginning, ramble from point to point, and end abruptly. If this were the case, students would more than likely be guessing their way through everything we as instructors attempted to teach. As a result of such disorganization, very little learning would probably take place. To keep our instruction clear and meaningful to others, normally it is necessary to organize it into steps with some logical progression. Step-by-step planning and presentation of this plan through instruction, if done correctly, is not easy, but is essential *if* our message is to be received and understood by others.

A handbook such as this could be used in a variety of ways: the most useful would be to read the one chapter of interest and then the others as time permitted; however, if this were done, one of the most important steps might be omitted—storyboarding and scripting, which *must* come first. *All* of the processes which are described in chapters two through five have as their origin a first step: storyboarding and then scripting. Just as an instructional lesson must have a beginning, so must *all* of the nonprint production items discussed in this book.

Much time can be lost, wasted, etc., if for some strange reason you choose *not* to read this chapter first. Backtracking to this particular chapter from all others in the handbook may leave you with many frustrated co-workers. So, have storyboarding and scripting "under your belt" *before* beginning.

After reading through the step-by-step approach to storyboarding and after examining the sample format, you should be ready to tackle any one of the other four chapters with ease and success, no matter how limited a background you have with 35mm cameras, still photography, video recording, or dry mount presses. The organization you derive from mastering storyboarding should give you enough confidence to learn how to produce the items right along with others—and enjoy it at the same time.

OBJECTIVE

To learn the basic techniques involved in storyboarding and scripting a nonprint program.

STRATEGIES

One of the best ways, if perhaps not the best, to learn this basic technique is to do it! Therefore, as you read through the procedure, you are invited, encouraged, *urged* to try to storyboard and script a topic, no matter how simple or ridiculous you may think it is. If you work through each step, this should give you the confidence to try the technique with a group.

DEFINITION OF TERMS

Storyboarding: A process whereby the idea or subject to be developed is broken down into small segments which can be rearranged until a desired, logical sequence is obtained; the individual segments usually contain some type of visual representation of what is to be seen, the *proposed* written script, if any, that accompanies the visual, and any particular instructions peculiar to that segment, such as the angle of the camera when taking the picture, music background, and desired volume/tone of the audio.

Scripting: The process of transferring the individual pieces of information from the storyboard cards onto a divided page where the visual is described and the narration is written out for each segment to be viewed; the two or three pages of script may be photocopied for distribution to the group for further reference.

Video: The picture to be visualized on the storyboard cards.

Audio: The written message or "script" that will accompany the visual on the storyboard cards.

MATERIALS AND COSTS

Storyboarding is an inexpensive activity in comparison with the nonprint productions covered in chapters two through five. The only expense to be anticipated is the cost for pencils, 5x8-inch note cards, and thumbtacks. You should not buy cards smaller than 5x8 inches since you will need the space for a rough sketch of the subject to be visualized, the accompanying script, and any special instructions. If you are working with a group of thirty other individuals, you will probably want around three cards for each so that they can practice with the limitations of space on two of the cards and finally produce one that is suitable. Once *you* have tried your hand at this, you will be convinced that three cards per individual is a minimum expenditure.

Item	Estimated Cost
5x8-inch note cards	under $1.50
box of #2 pencils	under $2.00
thumbtacks	under $1.00
Total	under $4.50

PROCEDURE FOR PRODUCTION

The procedure section, although long, is a detailed, step-by-step account of the process involved in compiling the information on a particular topic for nonprint production. The following steps are discussed: selecting the subject or idea, outlining the subject, storyboarding, and scripting.

A. Selecting the subject or idea

Perhaps the most difficult part of working through this activity and in producing any nonprint item in this handbook is deciding on the subject, the idea to develop. I have witnessed 50-50 splits in a group regarding the decision over which subject to storyboard that could never be resolved no matter how resourceful I was.

For your own protection and for the sake of group time, some pre-decisions need to be made by the person guiding the activity (teacher, media specialist, or elected student): have some suggested subjects, topics, and ideas ready for consideration, and keep these suggestions *simple*. By having a number of ideas ready, you immediately give the impression that some forethought has gone into the activity. You may even be surprised that the group likes one of the ideas and is willing to give it a try. However, no matter how innovative or creative you think your ideas are, it is *always* good to allow the group to express what it wants to do, what it needs to learn, or what it is *interested* in gaining from the experience. If you are able to maintain the group's *interest* in the first project of storyboarding, you might be able to *guide* participants later on to select a subject for development about which they want to learn more.

Another important point that merits a brief explanation is the need to keep *especially* the first storyboarding attempt as simple as possible. The whole idea behind using this technique is to be able to see, when completed, the entire presentation from start to finish, segment by segment, and to be able to identify any problems along the way *before* production begins. If you and/or your group makes the decision to tackle something too complex, you will become lost in a maze of a thousand-and-one storyboard cards that have very little meaning. Also, you will end up spending too much time on the technique, and interest in the final production might become seriously deflated. DECIDE ON A SIMPLE IDEA TO DEVELOP – at least for the first production.

Another consideration that must not be overlooked is the availability of materials for the chosen subject. If you are familiar with the resources of your media center, you have no problem; however, if you are not, have a media specialist present at your initial meetings to react to the variety of proposals. There is little reason for students to become excited over an idea if limited information or equipment is available. Also, by having the media specialist available for comment, this will alert him or her to reserve the desired materials *before* the actual research on the topic begins.

B. Outlining the subject

Once a group decision has been made to proceed and develop a specific subject, additional decisions need to be made before storyboarding begins. Using the input from the entire group, outline the subject. Decide on a tentative title. List the objectives to be accomplished within the framework of the presentation. Making such a list should give you and your group a clearer idea of exactly what it is you wish to show visually and to write for the content. Decide on your audience. Are you putting together a presentation on a particular subject for the group, for younger individuals, or possibly for parents or administrators to receive information? Such a decision needs to be made at the outset so that the content will be suitable for its audience. When you and your group have the following in front of you:

> Title:
> Objective(s):
> Audience:

you are ready to begin breaking the subject or idea down into its segments in outline form –

    I.
        A.
            1.
            2.
        B.
        C.
            1.
            2.

II.
    A.
    B.
        1.
        2.
            etc.

C. Storyboarding

Now that your outline is complete, you and your group are ready to begin storyboarding.

Steps
1. Pass out three cards and have each individual divide the cards into sections so it looks like this:

Video	Audio	#
Special Instructions:		5″

8″

By having each card identical, the entire unit when placed in proper sequence will be easier to visualize from beginning to end.

2. Explain what is meant by the different divisions:
    a. video—the picture
    b. audio—the written message that goes with the picture
    c. #—the number in pencil of the card so that it may be kept in sequence.
    d. special instructions—space allowed for any special effects desired, such as directions for taking the picture—close-up, head only, dissolve from one visual to another—or for recording with one or two voices or with a music background.

Warn the group at this point *not* to begin filling in their cards since no decision has been made as to *who* will be responsible for *what* on the outline.

3. Return to the outline. If the outline is too long or involved to be kept on the board, then a copy of it should be made available to each individual. It is a good idea to hand out these copies or record the outline so that, once the areas of responsibility for a particular segment are divided up, each individual knows which segment comes before and after his or her segment.

4. Verbally visualize the outline beginning with the first major point. By "verbally visualize" I mean ask and/or suggest pictures that would represent what is stated in the outline at present. Once a decision has been reached as to what should be visualized, ask for a volunteer to sketch the picture (no elaborate drawing in color or a photograph is necessary at this stage).

You will more than likely have a variety of comments regarding the student's inability to draw anything. *Reaction*: "So what!" You are not asking for a masterpiece; a stick figure is suitable. The storyboard is merely a sketch of the final product and is only to be used for guidance to check for the flow of ideas over your chosen subject. It is important that everyone become involved in this initial stage. The process encourages group interaction and the sharing of ideas in order to complete the finished production.

5 . Assign each individual an "A," "B," "C," etc., under each roman numeral until all segments are assigned (if you have subdivided the sections into "1," "2," "3," then these should be assigned one per person). Encourage the group to use all three cards to develop their pictures. Some may feel that an "A" or "B" needs to be subdivided into additional subunits; perhaps this is the case and three pictures are needed to deliver the message. However, also encourage them to write out the "audio" which describes their picture(s), especially if they subdivided the units, and to create additional visuals not covered in the outline.

No hard and fast rule exists regarding the number of sentences or words in those sentences used to describe a picture. If a paragraph is needed to describe one idea or segment, then more than likely this paragraph should be broken down into two or three sentences, each with an appropriate picture. If the medium to be used to display your pictures is slides, then a viewer may become bored by watching one slide while listening to an entire paragraph. On the other hand, if motion is being used, such as with television, then a paragraph may be needed in order to include the total motion demanded in that particular segment. This is where judgment comes into play *and* a willingness to experiment with the medium selected for the presentation.

Individuals may need more than three cards to work out their segments. If this is the case, they should be encouraged to ask for more until they are satisfied with their work.

6. Allow for plenty of in-class and/or out-of-class work time on this first stage. Creativity should *not* be rushed! Also, be prepared for the noise.

I have found that most individuals in a group setting become very excited over such projects and to "sit on" such enthusiasm would definitely be a mistake. Once one card has been completed, they will want to share the results of their labor with a neighbor or "check it out" with the group leader. They should also be encouraged to consult with the individuals whose segments come before and after their segment to make sure their picture-script (video-audio) agrees with others and is in sequence.

I am sure by now that you recognize the ease with which such a project as storyboarding could be accomplished by one person — you may want to storyboard an idea of your own *before* attempting the process with a group. However, the projects presented in this handbook are intended for exploration by a group. Hopefully, if you have the confidence to use these techniques, you will readily become convinced by the enthusiasm generated by students or others that a group encounter is ultimately more worthwhile and rewarding.

7. Once that *first* draft of cards is completed (warning: there will be many more *drafts* before the final project is viewed), thumbtack the cards on a bulletin board using the outline as a guide for sequencing. When all of the cards are in place, you may want to record a sequence number *in pencil* in the upper right-hand corner next to #.

Some people prefer to use a complicated coding system, such as I.A., I.B.(1), etc., which is unnecessary. A simple 1, 2, 3 ... is all that is really needed. You may want to have a lead card with the main divisions noted to help check on the balance of the presentation; i.e., I, II, III or Section I, Section II, Section III. Again, the number of cards within each division or segment will depend on your judgment and that of the group. This balance, or lack of it, is easier to see once the cards are displayed on the bulletin board. If you are doing a story, you may only need a brief beginning and ending — a few cards — and more in the body of the story — a larger number of cards. Practice — and a few mistakes — will help you judge how many cards to use with the selected topic.

8. Leave the storyboard alone in its rough form for a few days. Ask the students to read and view what is displayed to check for transition from picture to picture and from written text to written text.

If the finished product is to move from one point to another as smoothly as possible, this step is essential. By leaving the cards up for all to see, problems will become obvious.

9. After the group has had time to react individually, bring them together for a step-by-step inspection of each individual segment of the storyboard.

You may think that such time is wasted with both of these two steps; however, time spent at this stage will ultimately save hours later on, once the actual shooting of the visuals and taping of script begins.

Anticipate the noise! You have allowed for thinking time; now each individual will need to be heard. As you proceed from the first card to the last, be willing to move the cards from their original positions to other locations. It is wise *not* to remove any numbers recorded in the upper right-hand corner until you have made the *final* decision to leave the story-board *as is*. You may also find it necessary during this process to add to the cards already displayed or to delete some as the group decides on the development of the topic.

10. The decision must be made! There is no way that you will ever be able to please the entire group regarding the order of the storyboarding cards. If the majority agree, then you should stop the rearranging, renumber for proper sequencing, and begin writing the script.

D. Scripting

For scripting to be consistent, it is best to either solicit or assign a committee. Kemp and Dayton, in *Planning & Producing Instructional Media*, call the script "your detailed blueprint; the map which gives definite directions for your picture-taking, art work, audio recording, or video recording and filming" (p. 50). This is exactly what it is – a map which must be completed *first* before any decision is made on the visuals to be used. Realizing that realistically not everyone can be involved in the process, it is a good idea to allow the "art" committee, the "photographic" committee, and the "taping" committee to begin making preliminary plans so they will be ready with their contributions once the scripting is completed. Decisions about the medium to be used, the props to be set up or made, and the equipment operation that must be understood and tested – all are items which should be worked on before the script committee is ready to share its results.

One of the main reasons for having a script committee is to make the wording — the written manuscript — consistent in form. It is frequently at this stage that frustration sets in. This is the right time for the leader to have some of the answers to these frustrations.

Most individuals are usually *extremely* enthusiastic when it comes to working on a production such as this; however, once they face their own limitations in developing a topic so that it is factually correct, they are bound to become frustrated if they are not aware that the information they need is probably in print — books, reference materials, the vertical file, or periodicals — just waiting to be read. If the script committee has such a problem, this is the proper time for you to visit the media center. This is an excellent stage at which to bring the production wheels to a grinding halt for *all* committees and schedule a few research days. The script committee should be encouraged to share its problems and make the necessary assignments where information needs to be found before the script can be completed.

When students are working on such a project, they should be reminded that information they need on the topic should be placed in their own words and that they should copy down their sources and page numbers in case the script committee needs to check the information later. Also, they should be asked to describe briefly any visual contained on the printed page in case the art committee needs help or a point of reference for drawings or photographing this section.

A number of individuals react rather negatively to the word "research" when trying to apply it to students or varying ability levels. The bright or average student will, in all likelihood, not experience much difficulty at this stage; however, those who have a reading problem or who are, for some reason, reluctant to become involved need to be encouraged. For such students I have actually had to sit down and read to them and then ask them, in turn, to repeat in their own words what was read. Once they have understood the passage, together we write down the content for the script committee. The rewards of such patience are numerous. These individuals feel that they are still very much a part of the group activity and are contributing with a report on their findings. They are also the ones who, as a result of such a positive experience, are not nearly as reluctant to ask for help or who will willingly express a desire to have another and yet another passage explained to them when trying to discover information on their own.

SAMPLE FORMAT FOR STORYBOARDING

A. Selecting the subject or idea

1. How to make an apple cobbler	too complex; break this down into parts and select one
2. Techniques for peeling an apple	simple; can be broken down into small segments; a good beginning activity to learn storyboarding

B. Outlining the subject

Title: Techniques for peeling an apple	only a working title which may change a number of times before the final production

Objectives:
To show a variety of ways an apple can be peeled

To help others learn how to safely use sharp objects

To peel an apple so that it can be eaten or used for cooking.

List all of the objectives suggested. These will change and be refined once a direction is clarified by the group.

Audience: Elementary students: 2nd and 3rd grades

This will help the group determine the terminology to be used for the actual presentation.

Outline

I. Items needed—preparation—first step
   A. Apple
   B. Tools
      1. towels
      2. apron
      3. knives
      4. peelers

The first outline is a brainstorming experience in which everything is listed as fast as the group thinks of it. Rearrangement can take place afterwards.

II. The technique
    A. Peeling
        1. holding the apple
        2. which end do you begin with?
        3. care in handling the tools

    B. Cutting the apple
        1. remove the core
        2. reasons for cutting
           a. eating
           b. cooking

III. The cleanup
    A. Disposing of the peeling and core
    B. Cleaning the counter and utensils

IV. Eating the results

When the outline is complete, the group needs to reexamine the audience and the objectives to be accomplished, and select a title that adequately represents the topic. The final outline which you and your group produce should be refined enough so that it will not have to be reworked when the storyboarding begins. For this reason, I have found that when developing a topic such as this (and there are a variety of very simple ones to be developed), it is always best to *do* it with the class before making any revisions on the outline. Actually have one of the students visualize and verbalize the process in front of the class to check the outline on the board.

A refined outline might look something like this:

Title: The Apple: Peel it ... eat it ... but be safe in the process!

Objective: To show how to peel an apple and be safe at the same time.

Audience: Second- and third-grade students.

I. Preparation
    A. Gathering the items
        1. towels
        2. apron
        3. knife
        4. dish
        5. apple

    B. Cleaning the apple
        1. wash
        2. dry

II. Process
    A. Peeling the apple
    B. Quartering the apple
    C. Cutting out the core

III. Final stage
    A. Eating
    B. Cleaning up
       1. throwing the peeling and core away
       2. washing utensils

C. Storyboarding

One of the completed cards might look like this:

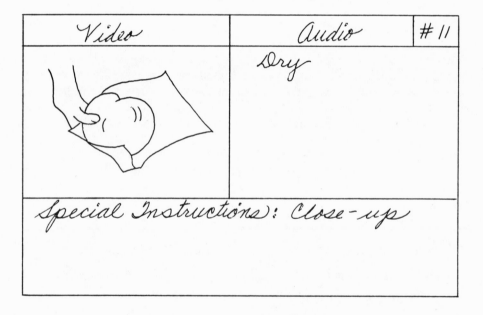

When displayed on the bulletin board, it is easier to see the entire development of the topic from beginning to end:

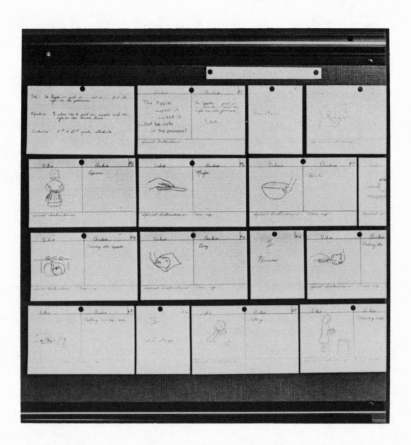

D. Scripting

Visual	Narration
1. Title: The Apple: Peel it … eat it … but be safe in the process!	The Apple: Peel it … eat it … but be safe in the process!
2. PREPARATION	Certain steps need to be considered before eating an apple. This is known as preparation.

(Continued on page 14.)

Visual	Narration
3. Person looking in cabinet for items.	If you decide to peel an apple, there are a number of items you will need before you begin.
4. Close-up of hands holding paper towels.	You will need paper towels to dry the apple.
5. Person putting on apron.	To protect your clothes, you might want to put an apron on.
6. Close-up of hands holding a kitchen knife.	You need to be very careful when handling the knife you will use to peel the apple.
7. Close-up of hands with bowl.	You should also have a bowl of some type to catch the peelings and core of the apple once you begin.
8. Apple on counter.	Last, but not least, you need the apple.
9. Person standing at sink with water running.	Before peeling the apple, it is a good idea to clean it thoroughly.
10. Close-up of water running over the apple.	Wash the apple with water to remove any dirt or insect spray.
11. Close-up of using a towel to dry the apple.	Take the towels you have placed beside the sink and completely dry the apple.
12. PROCESS	Now you are ready for the process of peeling the apple.
13. Close-up of hands holding the apple and knife.	Hold the apple firmly and peel it with the knife, starting at the stem end and moving slowly around the other side. Take your time and be careful to cut the apple and not your fingers.

Visual	Narration

14. Close-up of apple split in half and hands holding one section with a knife half way down on the section. | Once the apple has been peeled, cut the apple into two equal sections and then again into quarters. This will make it easier to remove the core where the seeds are.

15. Close-up of hands holding one section while removing the core. | Take each quarter and cut out the core or center of the apple.

16. FINAL STAGE | You are ready for the final stage of the process.

17. Person eating a section of the apple. | You can now enjoy eating the apple you have taken such care to peel.

18. Long shot of person carrying bowl and utensils to the trash. | You should not forget that cleaning up is also part of the process.

19. Person emptying peelings and core into trash can. | Throw the peeling and core into a trash can.

20. Person standing at sink washing the bowl and the knife. | The final step is washing the dish and the knife. Again, be careful not to cut your fingers when washing the knife.

Notice that the description of the visuals listed in the script are taken from the sketches on the storyboard (video) which have been developed from the ideas listed in the outline. The actual narration (audio) which will accompany the visuals is also an expansion of the outline. Care should always be taken to keep the grade level(s) and the specific objective(s) in mind when writing the narration for the presentation. Such a production could ultimately become a filmstrip with an audiotape, a slide/tape, or a brief television show. The format and equipment to be used will depend, to a great extent, on your willingness to experiment with various media.

SUGGESTIONS FOR FOLLOW-UP ACTIVITIES

The following topics, some of which demand a certain amount of research before they can be completed, are only suggestions for an initial investigation with storyboarding. Again, remember, the best experience is the one which is simple.

Primary

Sharpening a pencil
Constructing a puppet
Differences and similarities
Planting a garden
Making ice cream

Intermediate

Frying an egg
Washing dishes
Changing seasons
Metric measures
Planning a campout

Middle School

Cutting grass
Making a terrarium
Proper grooming
Parts of a book
From egg to chicken

High School

Writing a paper
Changing a tire
Development of a frog
Putting on makeup
Applying for a job

College

Physical fitness
Employment opportunities
Backpacking
Sorority/fraternity life
Visualizing a popular song

Note that the topics progress in degree of difficulty; some are suitable for younger children and others for young adults — your group's interests will help to determine the best topic to storyboard.

TAPPING LOCAL RESOURCES

1. In almost every community there is a newspaper. Editors, journalists, and cartoonists use storyboarding and scripting every day in order to produce the final copy which becomes a newspaper. An invitation to one of these individuals to speak to the group on their techniques for mapping the layout for either a story, a cartoon, or the entire paper might be meaningful for students to see the importance of this first step. If an actual visit to the newspaper building is possible, this would be appropriate after the initial presentation to understand how many individuals are involved in putting together one simple story in an entire paper.

2. If you are fortunate enough to have any book illustrators in your area, most would be willing to show the storyboarding and scripting they do before ever beginning the final production.

3. Graphic artists that work in business and/or television typically begin with a storyboard sketch that is shown to a client before scripting and before spending additional time and money on a project that might not meet a specific need. A presentation by such an individual, who would be willing to explain the process and display examples with the finished product, would be meaningful for any group to hear.

SOURCES FOR EQUIPMENT AND SUPPLIES

In the case of storyboarding, the items needed — pencils, 5x8-inch cards, and thumbtacks — can be purchased from almost any book or discount store. In many instances, the school stocks most of these.

A product that might be useful when first beginning is the "Audio Image Planner" (see illustration below), obtainable from Visual Horizons, 180 Metro Park, Rochester, NY 14623-2666. Their storyboard arrangement

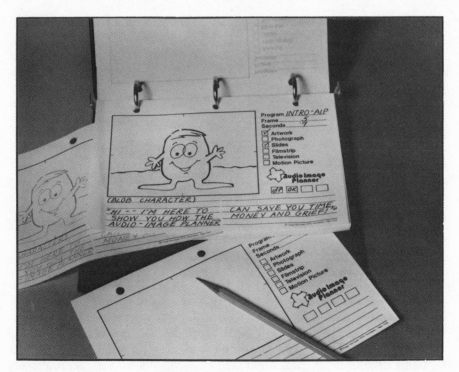

Courtesy of Visual Horizons

is essentially the same as discussed in this chapter, yet they have a ring binder which holds the 5½x8½-inch pages together, and each page has an original and two carbonless pages which may be removed and displayed. The planner kit costs $12 and contains one binder and 100 carbonless and 100 bound pages.

ANNOTATED BIBLIOGRAPHY

Edmonds, Robert. *Scriptwriting for the Audio-Visual Media.* 2nd ed. New York: Teachers College Press, 1984.
   The author devotes individual chapters to radio, films, television, documentary, multi-image, and filmstrips and slides, providing an overview of each medium as well as sample scripts. Helpful hints on employment possibilities and the way to be a professional conclude the book.

Gilkey, Richard. "Designing Student Production Facilities." *School Media Quarterly* 2 (Spring 1974): 256-59.
   The author discusses the production space requirements in order to provide adequate room for students to make their own materials. Consideration is given to super 8mm, video, still photography, and audio production facilities.

Kemp, Jerrold E., and Deane K. Dayton. *Planning & Producing Instructional Media.* 5th ed. New York: Harper & Row, 1985.
   Detailed coverage is given to storyboarding as a technique to be used in all aspects of producing audiovisual programs, from writing objectives and developing an outline to using cards to visualize the script (pp. 47-54). An entire chapter titled "Designing the Media" is devoted to the subject. Pictures are included.

Klos, Thornton A. "Scriptwriting." *Educational Resources and Techniques* 18 (Spring/Summer 1978): 19-20, 22.
   The author explores the importance of the script and the scriptwriter in the successful completion of a presentation for any medium.

Turner, Philip M. *Handbook for School Media Personnel.* 2nd ed. Englewood, Colo: Libraries Unlimited, 1980.
   The author explains the role the media specialist plays in assisting with student productions and then discusses the steps to be followed in organizing the presentation (pp. 71-74).

Wittich, Walter A., and Charles F. Schuller. *Instructional Technology: Its Nature and Use.* 6th ed. New York: Harper & Row, 1979.
   A brief overview of storyboarding is given with particular emphasis on "pupil planning for film-making." Illustrations of the technique are included (p. 240).

2

Computer Graphics*

INTRODUCTION

Sprites and pixels, scanners and laser printers; are these words from a magical land or from outer space? No, these are words from the world of computer graphics. To most of us, computer graphics contains a little magic and a bit of science fiction. The magic of the programmer's mind and vision are revealed in the intricate and colorful graphics of today's computer programs. We can make use of this special graphics technology to teach, encourage and inspire our students.

We live in a world which is visually oriented, full of color and movement. So it is with our computer programs. The application of computer graphics is an integral part of the computer programs used by today's students and teachers. These programs, whether designed for computer-assisted instruction (CAI), tutorials, desktop publishing or computer literacy, make use of graphics. Computer graphics provide the visuals necessary to any quality program.

Most students are eager to work with computers. Motivation is not a problem. The colorful graphics available on most programs only serve to reinforce this eagerness. This feeling is not limited to students. Harry Helms in *The McGraw-Hill Computer Handbook* describes this feeling: "The instant appeal of computer graphics to users of all ages has helped it to spread into many applications and will undoubtedly guarantee its continued growth and popularity" (p. 20-4).

The world of computer graphics makes use of the rapidly evolving world of computer technology to create more lifelike and elaborate visual displays. These displays are presented on monitors, printers, slides and transparencies. Printed computer graphics have the advantage of being effective, convenient, and economical of both time and money when

---

*This chapter was contributed by Maureen White, Abilene, Texas.

compared to hand-prepared graphics. Robert Edmunds in *The Prentice-Hall Encyclopedia of Information Technology* provides additional information on the use and advantages of computer graphics (pp. 110-20).

Dublin and Kelman provide an understandable explanation of computer graphics in their textbook *Macmillan Computer Literacy*. They explain that graphic images on a computer screen are actually outputs of tiny dots of light on a grid. The more grid cells, or pixels (term for picture elements), the higher resolution a visual will have. Special hardware devices including light pans, graphics tablets, joy sticks or a mouse may be used to input images. The computer graphics program allows one to interact with the computer to draw, paint, and in a sense, create the graphics (pp. 176-82).

The production of graphics in most computer programs is quite complex. Some students who have the talent, inclination, and that spark of necessary logic, will want to learn how computer graphics can be produced. Most of us, on the other hand, use computer graphics without consciously thinking about how they are produced. We do not understand computer graphics, but we use them. We use them to teach, to produce banners and class signs, to chart class progress, to produce mathematically conceived pictures with a Logo program, or whatever the computer graphics programmer provides for us.

Programs designed to produce computer graphics must have printer capabilities to truly support the program. Printers, including those producing color, are becoming more reasonably priced. Even a high resolution laser jet printer should be within the budget of most school districts in the near future.

Therefore, the major concern of this chapter will be with computer graphics programs which make use of a printer to produce a hard copy. These programs make the transition from the abstract, to the visual, to that which can be touched. Of major importance, the student or teacher walks away with tangible, concrete results.

Although the focus of this chapter is on graphics programs that allow for print capabilities, it is not intended to deny the importance of visual graphics in any type of computer program. Leslie Eiser in "What Makes a Good Tutorial?" for *Classroom Computer Learning* (January 1988) states: "High-quality graphics and animation that amplify and explain content should be a requirement—not an option—in any tutorial program" (p. 44). This should also be true for any program designed for student use. Too many programs allow the graphics to become overpowering. They are sometimes misleading or oversimplified.

In evaluating any computer software program, the user should be aware of the graphics. Ask yourself these questions:

Do the graphics relate to the objectives I have for the program?

Do the graphics motivate the user?

Are the graphics accurate in representation, neither oversimplified, nor overdone?

Are the graphics appropriate to the age and experience of the user?

Program criteria were also listed in the September 1985 issue of *Computer Classroom Learning* in Eiser's article, "What's a Picture Worth?" Eiser's considerations for selecting a computer graphics program include the following:

1. Is it menu driven?

2. Does it have a variety of possible drawing modes?

3. Does it have magnification, mirror, and cut-and-paste modes?

4. Does it provide for a variety of colors and textures?

5. Is the text mode available?

6. How easy is it to edit?

7. What external devices are necessary?

8. What printers can be used?

9. Is the software compatible to my computer system?

10. Does the software support color printers?

Using the above criteria when selecting a computer graphics program will ensure the selection of a quality program. Do not forget to check review sources and the lists of award-winning computer programs. These two sources often point the way to high-quality programs.

OBJECTIVE

To learn to use or teach others to use a computer graphics program.

STRATEGIES

When selecting a computer graphics program, consider the objectives to be accomplished, the age and experience level of your users, and the amount of hardware available for use. Another concern is the location of the computers. Are they to be used in a classroom, in the media center, or in a computer lab? How many students will be working at one time? The when, where, how, and with whom, must be addressed before planning a strategy for the use of a computer graphics program.

The objective for using a computer graphics program is of major importance. Is the program meant to teach computer literacy or to develop a better understanding of computer graphics? Perhaps it will accomplish both objectives. Some graphics programs are an end unto themselves. If a student or teacher wishes to produce a banner or sign, then the product becomes the objective. However, teachers and media specialists generally have additional objectives in mind when using a graphics program.

Is the primary objective for using a graphics program to produce announcements, banners, greeting cards, a class newspaper, Halloween masks, geometrical drawings or graphics for a class presentation? Education and computer periodicals provide reviews and teaching suggestions for quality graphics software. You do not have to guess about quality.

Make your first use of computer graphics one that will provide a successful experience for you and for your students. Don't start with a complex program that will only lead to frustration. When you start with a simple graphics program, it is easier to proceed to the more complex and creative programs. Remember this principle: easy to slightly more complicated to hard.

The primary concern of the student, media specialist or teacher is to have a *successful* hands-on experience. The choice of a simple graphics program which allows for easily understandable interaction is essential. The student should leave the experience with a feeling of success and a visible printed item in hand.

Identify the age or grade targeted for use with the computer graphics program. Does it require reading from the screen or a manual? Ideally the computer graphics program will be used after an introduction or demonstration followed by hands-on supervision. Select a user-friendly program which requires a minimum amount of instruction.

Be aware of necessary equipment, software, and materials to support a particular graphics program. Do you have special paper, ribbons, or colored markers available? The necessary items should be on hand and ready to use. It cannot be overstated: software and hardware must be compatible.

One does not need to be a computer expert to use a program written for students. However, be sure to run the program personally before introducing it to students. Get the bugs out! Anticipate any problems or questions that will arise or any difficulties your students may have. During the introduction and demonstration you will want to discuss any possible problems that might help to eliminate points of frustration to your students or to yourself.

Have examples of the computer graphics finished product available for students to view. Explain that their product may look slightly different. Using the finished example as an illustration provides the conceptualization necessary for elementary students.

Introducing a computer program to an entire class is not satisfactory if students have to wait days before using the program. It is best to introduce the program to students as they have access to a computer. The introduction can be either one-on-one or in small groups.

It is assumed that students will have used a computer before using a simple graphics program. If students are in the primary grades, it usually works best to have the computer program loaded in advance. Have the student's monitor turned off during the introduction. When the demonstration and introduction are completed and students are ready to work, turn the monitor on and stand back.

DEFINITION OF TERMS

Computer Graphics Program: Computer software designed primarily to produce a graphic or pictorial display.

Computer System: Consists of a central processing unit (CPU), monitor, and keyboard which are connected to work as one unit.

Laser Printer: Printer using laser beams to produce images with high resolution.

Scanner: Translates text, photographs, and art work into computer language to be stored and reproduced on the screen or printer.

Pixels: Points of light which depict computer images; the more pixels on the screen, the better the resolution.

Sprites: Programming techniques which facilitate computer animation graphics; smoother looking animation results and less memory is needed when using sprites.

MATERIALS AND COSTS

Computer hardware is expensive, but it is much more affordable than in the past. As technology has provided more advances in computers, more computers have been sold and prices have decreased. A color monitor is preferable with a computer graphics program. A color printer is also preferred if one with quality resolution and color is available. As the technology of color printers advances, better and less expensive models should become available. Color printers are presently affordable for schools. In the near future, laser printers should be within the budget of most school districts. Be sure to purchase hardware and software from reputable dealers who will quickly repair or replace broken equipment.

High-quality computer graphics programs range in cost from $50 to $500. Computer disks sell for approximately $0.25 to $3.00 each.

SUMMARY LISTS OF ESTIMATED COSTS

Equipment

Item	Estimated Cost
Computer System	$1000
Central processing unit (CPU)	
Monitor (color)	
Keyboard	
Printer	
Dot Matrix	300-800
Letter-quality	500-1500
Jet	2000-5000

Software and Supplies

Item	Estimated Cost	
Computer Graphics Program	$75.00	(average)
Supplies		
Printer Paper (box)	30.00	
Printer Ribbon	7.00	
Computer Disks (box of 10)	12.00	
Special colored paper/		
envelopes (180/60)	25.00	

OPERATION CHECKLIST FOR COMPUTER GRAPHICS PROGRAM

Each computer program and type of hardware has different procedures for use. This checklist is only a general guideline. Hardware and software manuals should be used for specific instructions.

Checkpoints	Satisfactory	Unsatisfactory
1. Set up computer system		
a. attach components	———	———
b. plug in	———	———
2. Prepare additional backup disks		
a. format the disks	———	———
b. label the disks	———	———
3. Assemble supplies		
a. colored ribbons	———	———
b. colored paper	———	———
c. markers/crayons	———	———
4. Prepare printer		
a. load with paper	———	———
b. turn on	———	———
5. Load program		
a. turn on monitor and computer	———	———
b. complete system setup (if required)	———	———
6. Run graphics program		
a. read instructions	———	———
b. select desired graphics	———	———
7. Print graphics		
a. check position of paper	———	———
b. tear carefully along perforation	———	———
8. Remove disks from computer		
a. place disks in protective cover	———	———
b. label and store	———	———
9. Completion		
a. turn off computer/printer	———	———
b. cover equipment	———	———

PROCEDURE FOR PRODUCTION

Experience shows that it is best to begin with a simple graphics program such as Print Shop™ (Broderbund, 1985). By beginning simply, students of all ages can easily see the possibilities of graphics. The idea is to help students use prepared graphics, but also give them the confidence that they can produce their own graphics. (Print Shop allows this option.)

Advance planning is essential before using a computer graphics program just as it is in any teaching situation. The teacher must actually load the program, run the program, and then print a final product in order to have examples of the finished product available. Students can then refer to these examples as they progress throughout the program. The teacher can expect great interest on the part of the students and a number of the students may already be familiar with graphics programs much more sophisticated in nature.

To encourage students to go beyond the experimentation and recreational stage with computer graphics, some guidelines are in order for the library media specialist:

1. Work with a teacher to select a unit of instruction where the use of computer graphics will support instructional goals.

2. Plan the activity and product which will involve computer graphics.

3. Develop a storyboard for the production. Assign areas of responsibility, graphics to be produced, and reports to be made. You will want to consider the introduction, order of presentation, closing, and ways which the graphics are to be displayed.

4. Write the script.

5. Teach students how to use the computer program. Allow students to use the programs so that the "how-to" does not interfere with the production.

6. Produce the assigned computer graphics.

7. If color is desired, and is not available through the printer, use colored markers, colored printer ribbons, water colors, crayons, or colored paper to enhance the graphics. Be careful not to cover the graphics by excessive use of color.

8. Merge the graphics and script. Refine as needed.

9. Videotape or make color slides of the production or use a software package to make a slide show of computer screen graphics. If printed graphics are produced, prepare transparencies or enlargements for oral reports.

10. Students will need to practice before presenting. Practice in the room to be used for the presentation, if possible. This will allow time to correct any problems that may be discovered. If possible do not stop during the final rehearsal. Time the practice sessions so that an accurate time estimate can be obtained.

SAMPLE FORMAT

Computer graphics programs are often used to supplement or enhance storyboarding activities. Examples of graphics used include banners, credits, and graphs. However, there are computer graphics presentations that may be prepared by students using graphics programs.

Seven students in the third grade planned the following presentation using graphics from the Print Shop. This was a seven minute presentation to their class entitled "Christmas Symbols—Computer Style." The students chose two members to introduce and close the presentation and the five remaining students each presented one Christmas symbol. A time limit of one minute was established for each participant. With the aid of the computer lab teacher and the media specialist, the students developed the objectives for the production and planned the presentation.

The computer lab teacher introduced and demonstrated the use of the Print Shop. This was the first time for students to use this program, so it was decided to use only selected graphics in Print Shop, excluding the other graphics in the program. The Christmas graphics symbols and banners were produced in the computer lab. The banner and sign graphics options were selected to produce the graphics for the presentation.

The students were introduced to the use of borders and fonts, as well as the placement of the Christmas graphics symbols and backgrounds. The use of examples prepared by the lab teacher and a card showing the choices proved helpful to the students. If an elementary student is to use a computer graphics program in a classroom or media center, the same type of preparation by the teacher or media specialist is essential.

Colored printer ribbon was available for use in printing the banners and symbols. Most students printed with a red or green ribbon. Several attempts were made before students were satisfied with the appearance of their computer graphics. Color was then added by students to highlight selected areas of the signs and banners.

The third grade class was studying Christmas symbols used around the world. The classroom teacher planned time for the seven students to research their assigned symbols in the media center. The script for their chosen symbol was critiqued and approved by the media specialist. This approved script was then added to each student's storyboard card. The media specialist checked storyboard cards and gave suggestions. Students then participated in several rehearsals.

OUTLINE FOR USING COMPUTER GRAPHICS PROGRAM

A. Select Program
    a. The Print Shop
    b. Choose banner and sign options

B. Objectives
    a. Produce Christmas signs and banners with computer graphics program
    b. Research background of the selected symbol
    c. Prepare storyboard card to aid in organization of presentation of symbols
    d. Prepare script

C. Title of Program
    "Christmas Symbols — Computer Style"

D. Participants — seven third grade students
    a. Five students assigned to five Christmas symbols
        1. Wreath
        2. Presents
        3. Christmas Tree
        4. Bells
        5. Candle
    b. Two students assigned to banners
        1. Introduction — "Christmas Symbols"
        2. Closing — "Merry Christmas"

E. Audience — third grade class

F. Time — Five minutes

G. Additional considerations — Prepare bulletin board to display symbols after presentation
    a. Plan placement in advance
    b. Have staples and thumbtacks ready

STORYBOARD GUIDELINE FOR PRESENTATION

Video	Audio
"CHRISTMAS SYMBOLS" Banner held by two students not reporting; place on board after introduction.	Welcome to our presentation of Christmas Symbols—Computer Style. (Introduction of students, acknowledge computer lab teacher and media specialist; introduction of subject)
"WREATH" Student reporting holds symbol; then places on board at conclusion of report.	(Report on Wreath)
"PRESENTS" (Same as above.)	(Report on Presents)
"CHRISTMAS TREE" (Same as above.)	(Report on Christmas Tree)
"BELLS" (Same as above.)	(Report on Bells)
"CANDLE" (Same as above.)	(Report on Candle)
"MERRY CHRISTMAS" Banner held by two students not reporting; place on board at end of report.	(Closing remarks, wish all "Merry Christmas")

As each student presents, the banners and symbols are placed on a prepared bulletin board. When the presentation is completed, the bulletin board serves as a visual reminder of the learning experience.

SUPPLIERS OF HARDWARE AND SOFTWARE

Hardware

There are numerous producers and distributors of computer hardware. Discounts are often provided via school bid systems or directly from computer companies to faculty and students. Compare prices and services of several dealers before purchase decisions are made. Three of the major suppliers of computers to schools include:

> Apple Computer, Inc.
> (Contact your local Apple dealer)
> 1-800-538-9696
>
> IBM
> (Contact your local IBM dealer)
> 1-800-IBM-2468
>
> Tandy Computers
> (Contact your local Radio Shack)
> 1-800-433-5682
> 1-800-772-8538 (in TX)

Software

Computer graphics software is available through most hardware and software distributors. Most media centers have software catalogs of major distributors. Check replacement, support, and licensing of software before purchasing. Another good source is to ask students in the school. They often have good programs they can recommend, particularly if they have worked with a number of graphics programs and can compare one with a number of others. The following is a list of some of the major suppliers or producers of graphics software for schools:

> Baudville
> 1001 Medical Park Dr., SE
> Grand Rapids, MI 49506
> 1-616-957-3036
> Sample software: Take 1 (Apple)
>
> Berkley Electronic Publishing
> P.O. Box 3056
> Berkley, CA 94703
> 1-415-652-6004
> Sample software: Printmaster (Apple)
>
> Broderbund Software
> 17 Paul Dr.
> San Rafael, CA 94903
> 1-415-479-1700
> Sample software: Print Shop (IBM, Apple, Commodore, Macintosh); Fantavision (Apple); Dazzle Draw (Apple)

Claris
440 Clyde Ave.
Mountain View, CA 94043
1-800-334-3535
Sample software: MacDraw; MacPaint (Macintosh)

Data Transforms, Inc.
616 Washington
Denver, CO 80203
1-303-832-1501
Sample software: Fontrix (Apple, IBM)

Electronics Arts
1820 Gateway Dr.
San Mateo, CA 94404
1-415-571-7171
Sample software: Deluxe Paint II (Apple IIgs, Commodore,
    Amiga)

Mindscape Inc.
3444 Dundee Rd.
Northbrook, IL 60062
1-312-480-7667
Sample software: Bank Street Storybook (Apple)

Spinnaker Software Corp.
One Kendall Square
Cambridge, MA 02139
1-617-494-1200
Sample software: Kidwriter (Apple, Commodore)

Springboard Software, Inc.
7808 Creekridge Circle
Minneapolis, MN 55435
1-800-328-1223
Sample software: Newsroom (IBM, Apple)

SELECTED COMPUTER SOFTWARE
REVIEW SOURCES

The following is a list of some periodicals that regularly review computer software:

Booklist
Classroom Computer Learning
Electronic Learning
Instructor
Learning
School Library Journal
Teaching and Computers

SUGGESTIONS FOR FOLLOW-UP ACTIVITIES

1. Use additional graphics packages available with Print Shop to increase choice of graphics, e.g., Print Shop Companion or The Print Shop Graphics Library Holiday Edition.

2. Present reports of symbols of other holidays using computer-generated symbols.

3. Make greeting cards or bookmarks with graphics programs.

4. Use a combination word processing/graphics program, such as Kidwriter (Spinnaker 1984) to add text to graphics. It can easily be used by any student who can read.

5. Make Halloween masks for use with a Halloween play or just for fun with Mask Design (Springboard 1984). This is easy to use with any age student.

6. Prepare a class or school newspaper with computer graphics/word processing program such as The Newsroom (Springboard 1985). See the May/June, 1987 issue of *Teaching and Computers* for an excellent outline for using the program to produce a class newsletter or paper. Suitable for grades four and up.

7. If a color printer is unavailable, use color ribbons, paper, or color with pens, markers or crayons, if color will improve the final product.

8. Use a Logo program such as LogoWriter (Logo Computer Systems) or The Terrapin Logo Language (Terrapin, Inc.) to teach higher level thinking skills and mathematics and geometry concepts. Many computer periodicals appropriate for students or teachers provide monthly lessons using any Logo program. Students of all ages can use Logo programs.

9. Introduce the scanner concept using clip art. Show or share with a class how drawings or pictures can be saved and later reproduced by a computer graphics program. Arrange to have a scanner to show or use (Thunderscan produced by Thunderware is one such product).

TAPPING LOCAL RESOURCES

1. Have the class visit or be visited by a graphics artist to show the skills and techniques involved in manually producing graphics.

2. Visit a newsroom of a local newspaper's layout room. Compare the class newspaper produced by a program such as The Newsroom to the local newspaper.

3. Visit a computer store or have a representative visit your class to show the variety of computer graphics programs available.

4. Locate a local business which uses desktop publishing. Arrange for a representative to visit the class or have the class visit the business to show how desktop publishing is accomplished. Show samples of the results of desktop publishing.

5. If close to a local university campus, plan a visit to see the types of graphics programs being produced and used by these students.

6. Coordinate a day-long seminar where students from different schools can share ideas and learn.

ANNOTATED BIBLIOGRAPHY

Dublin, Peter and Peter Kelman. *Macmillan Computer Literacy*. New York: Macmillan Publishing Co., 1986, pp. 175-82.
This computer literacy textbook provides general information on the subject. Includes information on computer graphics.

Edmunds, Robert A. *The Prentice-Hall Encyclopedia of Information Technology*. Englewood Cliffs, N.J.: Prentice Hall, Inc., 1987, pp. 110-20.
Highly technical, comprehensive reference tool covering information on computer science and new areas of technology.

Eiser, Leslie. "Software Update," *Computer Classroom Learning* 7 (March 1987): 22-23.
Reviews updated graphics program, Create with Garfield! Deluxe Edition, which received a *Computer Classroom Learning* "Award of Excellence" in 1987.

Eiser, Leslie. "What's a Picture Worth?" *Computer Classroom Learning* 5 (September 1985): 64-68.
Criteria for selecting a computer graphics software program is presented. Compares major graphics programs.

Eiser, Leslie. "What Makes a Good Tutorial?" *Computer Classroom Learning* 8 (January 1988): 44-51.
Describes qualities of a good tutorial, including the power of interactive graphics.

Everhart, Nancy and Claire Hartz. "Creating Graphics with 'The Print Shop'," *School Library Journal* 31 (May 1985): 148-50.
Clear step-by-step procedure for using The Print Shop are presented. Suggested uses for other graphics options and packages are also given.

Greitzer, John. "Scanning the Horizon," *Publish!* 1 (September/October 1986): 45-51.
Discusses problems existing in desktop scanners and makes predictions for the future of scanners.

Harvey, Brian. "Finding the Best Logo for Your Students," *Computer Classroom Learning* 7 (April 1987): 41-47.
A comparison of popular Logo programs is made using established software evaluation criteria.

Helms, Harry. *The McGraw-Hill Computer Handbook*. New York: McGraw-Hill Book Company, 1983, p. 20-4.
This comprehensive computer handbook provides technical information on computers including computer graphics.

Kinnamon, J. C. "The Hi-Tech Where-to-Go Guide," *Instructor Special Hi-Tech Issue* 92 (Fall 1987): 24-26.
Provides a clip-and-save list of sources, software, people and places. Telephone numbers are provided for major software producers.

"Kids Create 'World's Largest Banner'," *Teaching and Computing* 4 (March 1987): 4.
Using The Print Shop, students produced a 1.7 mile banner. It has been submitted for a world record to *Guinness Book of World Records*.

"LogoWriter: The Turtle Wins the Race," *Incider* 4 (December 1986): 184.
Editor's Choice review of LogoWriter gives examples of how the program is used in classrooms.

Mandell, Phyllis Levy. "AV Programs for Computer Know-How," *School Library Journal* 31 (February 1985): 23-28.
AV software programs useful for explaining computer concepts are reviewed. Included are three computer graphics sound filmstrip kits.

McLanahan, Janet Fowle. "Software for Young Children," *Day Care and Early Education* 12 (Winter 1984): 26-29.
Reviews the types of software available to preschool children and ways it can be used in early childhood education programs.

Olivas, Jerry. "Laser Printers: Exotic Graphics and Other Eye-Catching Output for Under $3,000," *Computer Classroom Learning* 7 (November/December 1987): 49-53.
Discusses pros and cons of laser printers and how they work. The emphasis is on desktop publishing.

Rappaport, Susan. "Computer Graphics for the Novice," *Library Journal* 110 (September 1, 1985): 146-47.
Summarizes existing computer graphics programs, their strengths and weaknesses.

"Read All about It," *Teaching and Computers* 5 (November/December 1987): 23.
Useful computer ideas to use during Book Week are displayed on a large fold-out poster.

Revenaugh, Mickey. "End-of-the-Year Project," *Teaching and Computers* 4 (May/June 1987): 35-42.
Provides an excellent plan for using The Newsroom or similar desktop publishing software to produce a class newspaper. Designed for students in grades four and up.

Rosen, Marian. "But Wait, There's More," *Classroom Computer Learning* 7 (October 1987): 50-55.
Describes uses of award-winning LogoWriter for students of all ages.

3

Transparency Lifts and Lamination

INTRODUCTION

Making transparency lifts and laminating flat pictures are two techniques that I have found are always successful activities in developing confidence in individuals wanting to make their own materials. There is a real inward satisfaction gained when the individual is successful with lifting a clay-coated picture onto a piece of clear plastic film, or when laminating a series of drawings or even pictures from a magazine to form a story for others to see and/or use. The common responses that I have had when going through this activity with a group are: "I never dreamed I could do that," "It was so easy," "Let's do it again," "I've got to take it home to hang in my room," or "I can't wait to use this with my seventh-graders in our next science unit." Once you have tried either or both of these activities, I am sure you will agree with the above statements.

There are numerous other activities that could be covered which are related to transparency lifts and lamination (some of these are briefly discussed in the "Suggestions for Follow-Up Activities"). However, from past experience, you should try these activities first; if the enthusiasm continues, you might want to attempt the follow-up activities.

OBJECTIVES

To be able to laminate flat pictures for use in relating stories, a sequence of events, or a bulletin board display.

To learn how to lift color clay-coated pictures in order to make overhead transparencies.

STRATEGIES

Some of the individuals you might choose to take part in these activities will never have seen a transparency or a laminated picture. Therefore, showing them each item is important so they will have a frame of reference from the beginning. If you have a clear acetate sheet and transparency marking pens or if you have any type of clear plastic, such as plastic sandwich bags and some translucent paints, you can mark or paint on the plastic, hold it up to the light, and show the students how they can see through it. After this, place your markings onto the overhead projector, and display your creation on a screen or the wall.

After showing them how translucent configurations can be projected, take a clay-coated picture from a magazine (to test for clay coating, place a few drops of water on one corner of the picture and rub; if the picture does not dissolve and if a white, chalky residue comes up when gently rubbing the corner, then you probably have a clay-coated picture). Hold it up to the light—students will not be able to see through it. Place it onto the overhead projector—again, students will only see a black blob on the screen. Ask them why the picture cannot be projected—the answer should be obvious: the picture is not translucent; therefore, light will not pass through it!

If, at this stage, your group appears inquisitive and wants to know if projection of this picture is ever possible, explain that it is, but the process is really messy. If you did not have them interested before, you will now. There is nothing better to get a group excited than making a creative mess in the classroom or media center.

I use another approach to involve the group in laminating pictures. In my files I always keep drawings and cut-outs from magazines that have not been laminated but that have been used either in class for lecture-discussion periods or for bulletin boards. Usually I do not even have to comment on the condition of either—the edges of the pictures are frayed, some have been torn, and indeed some should never be used again considering their wrinkled condition. Is there a remedy for future use of pictures and/or drawings that I wish to keep on file for presentations? Yes. If you have a driver's license, your picture was probably protected by laminating film and this can be shown to the group. If you do not have such a picture on hand, almost all drug-discount stores have a machine that can laminate a picture which you can show to the class.

DEFINITION OF TERMS

Transparency lift: A method used to transfer a clay-coated picture onto clear plastic film so that the picture becomes translucent and can be projected on an overhead projector; the ink in the original picture is actually lifted onto the laminating film with heat and the clay-coated backing is washed away (see top photograph on page 38).

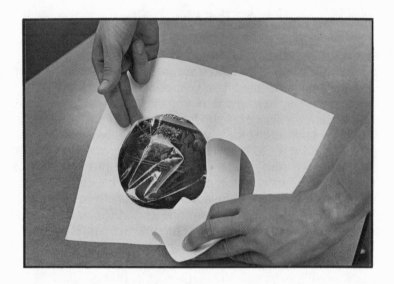

Lamination: A process whereby a picture or drawing is protected using a clear plastic film placed over the top of the original.

Laminating film: A clear plastic, heat-sensitive film which when heated to a recommended temperature will adhere to another surface; this particular kind of film may be used for transparency lifts or for lamination (see photograph on page 39).

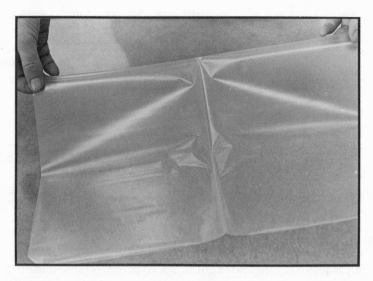

Dry mount press: A machine made especially for the dry mount and lamination process; the upper plate temperature may be regulated according to the process so that heat is evenly distributed over the item.

Dry mount tissue: A specially treated paper which when heated to a prescribed temperature melts the glue on both sides so that a picture or drawing will adhere to another surface such as posterboard or construction paper (see photograph below).

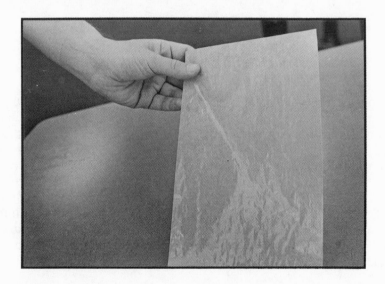

Tacking iron: A heating iron used to tack the dry mount tissue and the 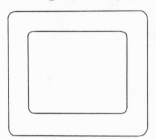 laminating film to the object before place-ment into the dry mount press; by using the tacking iron, you ensure that the tissue and film will not move.

Mounting frame: A precut cardboard frame with a display opening so that 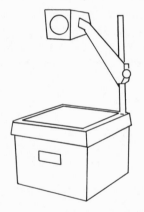 the transparency may be taped onto it for ease in handling and storage. Frames may also be handmade using a precut frame as a guide for tracing the inner outline onto thin 9x12-inch cardboard sheets and cutting the inside por-tion with a single-edged razor blade or scissors.

Overhead projector: A piece of equipment to project translucent materials 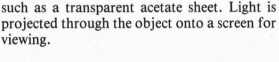 such as a transparent acetate sheet. Light is projected through the object onto a screen for viewing.

MATERIALS AND COSTS

The most expensive item to be purchased in the equipment line is the dry mount press. A variety of sizes are available; however, you need to determine which machine will meet your continued needs for dry mount-ing and laminating. The best advice is to buy the largest press that your budget will allow. If you are forced into choosing and your budget is limited, then strike a compromise and purchase the 12x15-inch size press for around $400. The overhead projector used to show your transparen-cies will range in price from $230 to $500. Other items in the equipment line include a tacking iron for $40, a good pair of cutting shears for around $2.50, and a couple of single-edged stencil cutting knives with extra blades for $1.35 each.

Supplies for these processes are not inexpensive, but if bought in sufficient quantity, money may be saved. Laminating film may be purchased by the roll; for example, a 11½-inch by 50-foot roll sells for $18. A variety of other sizes are available. Dry mount tissue may be bought by 100-sheet boxes or by the roll: $15. If care is taken to keep scraps and unused pieces in separate boxes, a group, if encouraged, will go to the scrap boxes first to complete the project. Posterboard is something that can be bought in a variety of widths and lengths and then cut to desired specifications. A single sheet of 28x44-inch posterboard sells for $1.75 to $2.00. If you want a cheaper and thinner posterboard which can be purchased in discount stores, a 22x30-inch sheet sells for about $0.50. Construction paper, masking tape, butcher paper (or newsprint), and mounting frames are other items listed on the summary sheet which should also be purchased.

SUMMARY LIST OF ESTIMATED COSTS

Equipment

Item	Estimated Cost
dry mount press	
12x15-inch (small)	$400.00
18½x15½-inch (medium)	650.00
18½x23-inch (large)	900.00
tacking iron	40.00
scissors	2.50
stencil cutting knife with blades	1.35
overhead projector	230.00

Supplies

Item	Estimated Cost
laminating film	
roll (11 1/8 inches by 50 feet)	$18.00
dry mount tissue	
box of 100 sheets (8½x11-inch)	15.00
posterboard (28x44-inch)	2.00
construction paper (50 sheets)	2.50
masking tape (1 roll)	1.50
mounting frames (1 box of 100)	17.00
butcher paper (1 roll)	2.50
cotton balls (1 large package)	2.00

OPERATION CHECKLIST FOR
THE DRY MOUNT PRESS

Checkpoints	Satisfactory	Unsatisfactory
1. Open the press; check for foreign matter on heating platen and bottom cushion; clean both if necessary.	_____	_____
2. Plug into wall.	_____	_____
3. Close press halfway while heating.	_____	_____
4. Set the temperature guide for process: dry mounting (225°); laminating (300°); or lifting (325°).	_____	_____
5. Allow time for the press to reach the set temperature (10-20 minutes).	_____	_____
6. Open the press and insert the material, making sure that it is covered with blank newsprint or butcher paper for protection.	_____	_____
7. Close the press.	_____	_____
8. Allow enough time for the object to seal (refer to manual).	_____	_____
9. Open press and remove object. Check for complete seal. If incomplete, insert object back into newsprint carrier and place into press for a longer period of time.	_____	_____
10. Turn press off and unplug.	_____	_____

OPERATION CHECKLIST FOR
THE OVERHEAD PROJECTOR

Checkpoints	Satisfactory	Unsatisfactory
1. Locate and set up screen for display.	_____	_____
2. Locate table or cart on which to place the overhead projector.	_____	_____
3. Plug overhead into outlet.	_____	_____
4. Place test transparency onto stage of overhead.	_____	_____
5. Turn overhead lamp on; adjust top mirror head onto screen; focus.	_____	_____
6. Move table closer to reduce or farther away from the screen to increase the size of the transparency image. Refocus if necessary.	_____	_____
7. Remove test transparency and store.	_____	_____
8. Unplug overhead projector and return to storage.	_____	_____
9. Remove screen.	_____	_____

PROCEDURE FOR PRODUCTION

It is very easy to begin making color lifts and to laminate pictures without any particular goal beyond simply mastering the two processes—this appears at first glance to be worthy in and of itself, and indeed it is; however, much, too much, laminating film can be and is wasted by over-learning both processes. It is much better to demonstrate the techniques using the step-by-step procedures discussed here and then begin working from the storyboard so that the activity will be completed within pre-established time and cost boundaries.

It is also very easy to have both lifting and laminating going on simultaneously since the same machine is used; however, be sure that you divide the room in half so that half the group is on one side and half on the other. You will be using water for lifting, and watermarks on pictures to be laminated are not attractive.

Dry Mounting a Picture onto Posterboard

1. Set the dry mount press on 225° (see manufacturer's instructions). Allow at least 5 minutes for the press to heat completely.

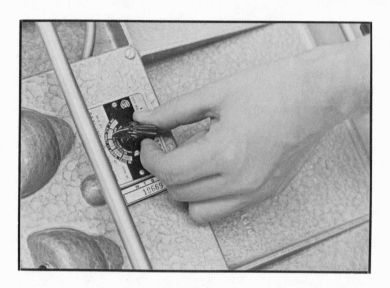

2. Find a picture printed on clay-coated paper or article from a newspaper and cut it out.

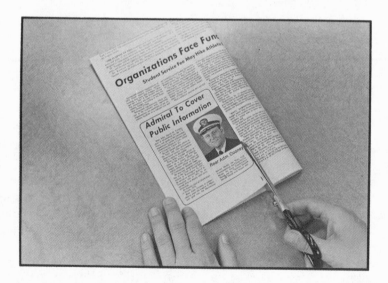

3. Tack a piece of dry mount tissue on the back center of the picture or article with the preheated tacking iron. The dry mount tissue should be slightly larger than the picture to be mounted.

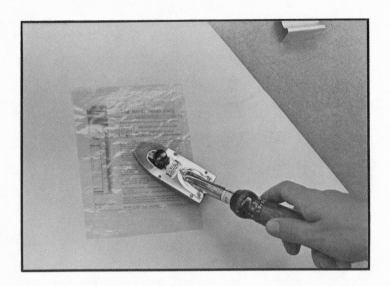

4. Trim the tissue and picture/article so that *no* tissue may be seen beyond the edges.

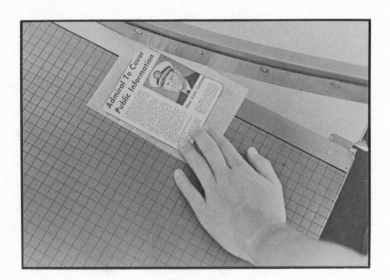

5. Place the picture/article on the posterboard and, holding the center in place with the fingers, lift up each side and tack the corners to the posterboard.

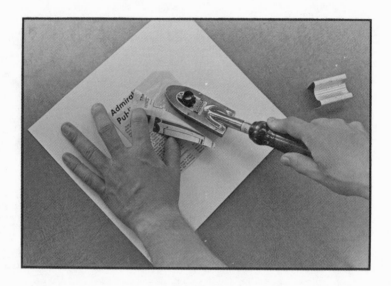

6. Slip the completed work between the butcher paper (or newsprint) to protect the posterboard and press.

7. Place the assemblage in the preheated 225° dry mount press for about 45-60 seconds.

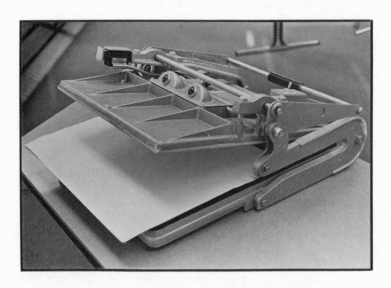

8. Remove. Check the edges for a complete seal between the picture/ article and the posterboard. If the seal is incomplete, place the material back into the press for another 45 seconds.

In humid areas, it is always a good idea to dry the pictures or articles before you begin to work; this removes all the moisture content. Simply place the item you wish to laminate and/or lift in the butcher paper in a preheated press of 180° for around 2 minutes, remove, and let cool. This simple step will greatly improve the quality of your work.

Laminating the Dry Mounted Picture/Article

1. Set the press on 300° and allow 5 to 10 minutes for it to heat.

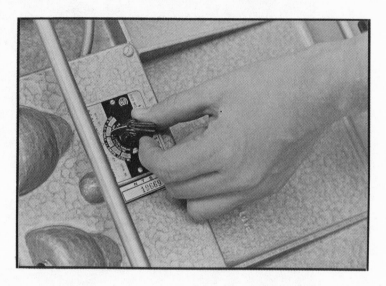

2. Using a piece of laminating film, cover the entire posterboard. Make sure the dull side is against the posterboard.

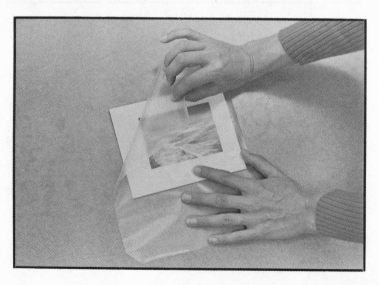

3. Tack the edges of the film with the tacking iron to the poster-board to hold it secure. Trim away excess film so that it will not adhere to the butcher paper.

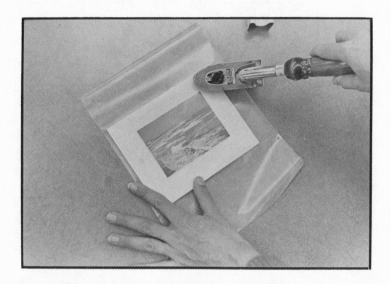

4. Insert the material between another piece of clean sheet of butcher paper for protection, and place in the press for around two minutes.

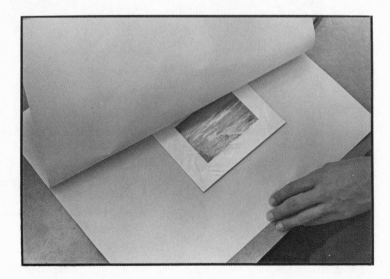

5. Remove and place under a weight *or* under a number of books so that the posterboard will remain flat while cooling.

6. Once cooled, trim away any additional edges of excess film.

If you have a dry mount press which has been used for a number of years, or even one that has not, you may want to increase the amount of pressure on the item you are laminating by lifting the bottom pad and placing a Masonite board or folded newsprint underneath. This will increase the pressure and should improve the seal between the film and the posterboard.

Color Lifting for Transparencies

1. Set the dry mount press for 325°. Allow 5 to 10 minutes for the press to heat.

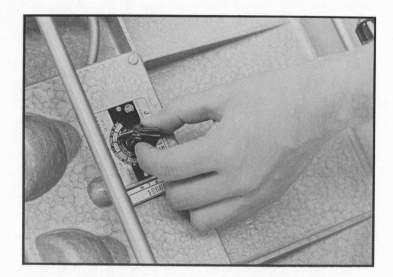

(Text continues on page 52.)

2. Select a clay-coated picture from older copies of magazines such as *National Geographic, People, Life*, etc. Test the picture on the side *not* to be lifted by rubbing a small amount of water on one corner. If a chalky residue comes up and the picture does not dissolve, it is clay coated. (See photograph below.)*

3. Trim the picture to the desired size, and cover with laminating film. Leave excess film beyond the picture for placement in the transparency mount frame.

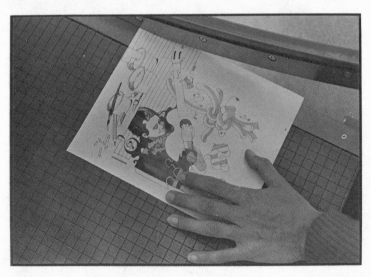

4. Tack the corners of the film with a picture underneath to the butcher paper to hold it secure. Remember to have the dull size of the film *against* the picture you wish to lift.

5. Sandwich this between a top and bottom layer of butcher paper and insert into the dry mount press for 2 minutes.

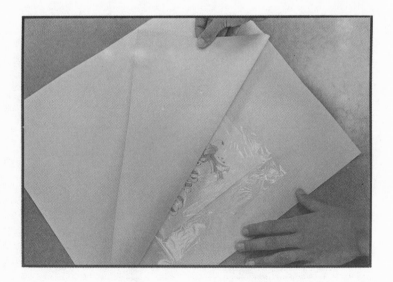

6. Remove from the press and the sandwich of butcher paper, and place the laminated picture into soapy water (the same in which you would normally wash dishes). Make sure the picture is completely immersed. Allow to stand for around 10 minutes.

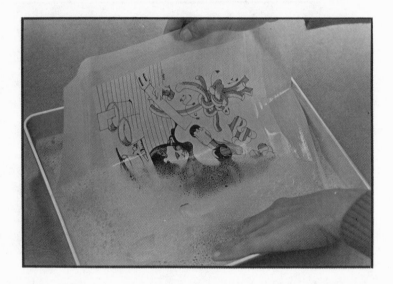

7. Take out of the water and gently peel away the butcher paper *and the picture*.

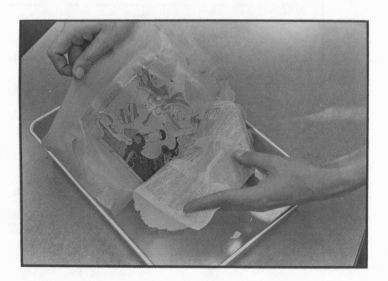

8. Remove the clay residue using clean cotton balls. Rub in a circular motion until completely cleaned. Wash the film under the faucet to remove the white chalky substance. Let dry completely by hanging with several clothespins.

9. When the lift is thoroughly dry, tape the shiny side down to a piece of thick cardboard. Using either a clear acrylic spray or a clear floor wax, spread an even, thin coat over the lift with the spray or a clean brush and let dry.

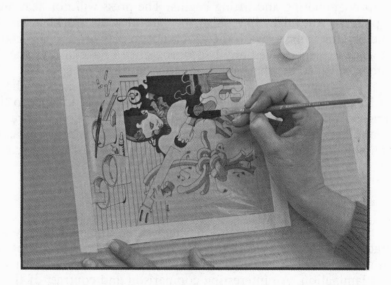

10. Remove from the cardboard and tape the lift onto a mounting frame. If the picture you have lifted is too small for a regular size mount, use posterboard and a single-edged razor blade or stencil cutting knife and cut out a frame that is the right size.

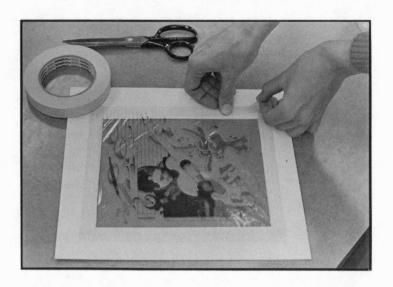

After reading through the above, you should have noticed that the dry mount press has to be set on different temperatures. If you have *two* presses, you will have no trouble; however, if only one is available, then you will want to first complete as much of the dry mounting as possible *before* laminating and lifting begins. The press will not heat and cool as rapidly as you might like. Also, be careful when working with the press and tacking irons to warn the group not to play around this equipment. I have never experienced any bad burns since I have always warned everyone in advance of what could possibly happen.

It is important to note that this procedure is messy. The mess can easily get out of control if the group is not advised in advance to clean up as much as possible as they progress through the steps. If the areas are kept clean, there is less likelihood that a most unusual color lift or an attractive laminated picture will be ruined by particles of dust or water spots.

SAMPLE FORMAT

The following presentation was written and planned by a seventh-grade world history class studying multicultural young people and their customs. Both procedures were used by the class—color transparency lifts and lamination. An interesting comparison and contrast of the strengths and weaknesses of both were attached after the project was completed.

TITLE: STUDENTS OF THE WORLD

PLANNING: Seventh-grade students had been studying different cultures and their particular customs for four weeks prior to the beginning of the project. Using pictures from discarded *National Geographic, Life, Time,* and other clay-coated magazines, students first read the article regarding the particular culture and then paraphrased it in their own words. The pictures were then cut from the magazines using single-edged razor blades.

         One week was set aside for the explanation and practice of making color transparency lifts and laminating. Half of the students decided to use one method for their reports and the other half wanted to make their reports in the form of a visual display for a bulletin board.

PROJECTS: Group #1 Color Transparency Lifts

         Students worked first in one large group and decided on which students would be responsible for which country. A limitation had to be made on the countries to be discussed since only clay-coated pictures could be used. Two individuals were responsible for storyboarding the project after the group discussion. After the second group meeting in which the storyboard was presented and finalized, each student worked up his or her script, decided on the picture or pictures to be lifted, and presented the idea to the entire group. Once the program had been approved, students lifted their pictures and made the transparencies. The entire group placed their narration on a cassette tape with a "ping" recorded to indicate the change from one transparency to another. One student from each group presented the project to the entire class. (Time to complete the activity: two weeks.)

TITLE: STUDENTS OF THE WORLD

PROJECTS: Group #2   Lamination

Students in this group decided to laminate pictures gathered from *one* country. All students met in a large group and selected one country that they felt needed further investigation. Two countries were picked and then an examination of pictures available was made. During the second meeting the students decided on "Students in Germany" to display, storyboarded their presentation as a group, and outlined their narration. Each student laminated his or her own pictures onto the same color and same size of posterboard. One student recorded the narration onto cassette tape, with a number in sequence preceding each picture description. The laminated display was pinned to the bulletin board with a lettered number placed to the lower right of each picture. The cassette recording was placed next to the display so that the other students could listen as a group or individually. (Time to complete the activity: two weeks.)

COLOR LIFTS:

Strengths	Weaknesses
1. Easy to store for future use.	1. Only clay-coated pictures could be lifted.
2. Easy to transport to other classrooms for presentation.	2. Some pictures were wasted since students did not get a perfect seal with the film.

STORY LAMINATION:

Strengths	Weaknesses
1. Easy to store and not easily damaged.	1. It was difficult to move to other classrooms.
2. A variety of pictures could be laminated — no restriction to clay base.	2. The display took up too much space; some pictures had to be taped to the wall.

— Barbara Harris

SUGGESTIONS FOR FOLLOW-UP ACTIVITIES

There are numerous activities directly related to making transparency lifts and lamination. The following are only a few ideas; you will want to experiment on your own as you gain confidence with these productions:

1. Now that you have lifted clay-coated pictures for overhead transparencies, you should try making slides using the same process. Remember that your choice of pictures will be restricted to a 1x1½-inch format for placement in cardboard or plastic slide-ready mounts. The mounts may be purchased in quantities to 100 for around $2.75 (cardboard)—$5.00 (plastic). Because the lamination film is flimsy, it will have to be stretched and taped onto the slide mounts, coated on the back with the clear acrylic wax, allowed to dry, and then sealed into the slide mount. An entire slide-tape presentation using the same procedure in this chapter may be developed.

2. Another activity which a group enjoys is drawing with transparency marking pens or paints directly onto the film. It is best to mount the film in the frames first to hold it steady and to cut down on the possibility of smearing the finished work. If you wish to trace maps or outlines of drawings onto the film, the film in the mount can be placed directly over the picture. If you use permanent ink or translucent paint, you will not have to worry about smearing the drawing; however, if you use ink that comes up when you touch it, then you will need to spray the finished product with a clear acrylic spray which may be purchased from local arts and crafts dealers. Or, you can cover the finished product with a clean, clear piece of transparency film and tape down all sides to protect the original.

3. A variety of items may be laminated if properly dried and flattened. Your group may wish to collect fall leaves or spring flowers and dry and press them first in the dry mount press. (Make sure you use butcher paper around the items to protect the press.) If you set the press on 180°, you may leave the collected item in for a few minutes to begin the drying process. Don't leave them in too long or the odor will be too strong for you to endure. Take them out and press them between old book pages—again, using butcher paper to keep the items from sticking to the pages. After a few days, dry and press them again in the press to remove all moisture. These may be laminated for display on the bulletin board.

4. I have used the lamination process repeatedly for protecting instructional units which I knew I would be using again and again. By placing a protective plastic cover over the top and bottom of the worksheet, messy fingers or recorded answers on a worksheet using a temporary felt-tipped ink pen or even a crayon may be wiped clean and reused. Teachers who have purchased expensive games, or who have taken the time to make their own, have found that laminating these *before* they are used increases their circulation. I have encouraged both younger and older students to make their own puzzles and games. Once a picture has been dry mounted to a cardboard or a posterboard backing and laminated on both sides, it may be cut into a variety of shapes for puzzle pieces.

5. An item which you might like to write for once you have made your own transparencies is "Polarmotion Overhead Transparencies" promotion kit from American Animation, Inc., 300 Mill Street, P.O. Box 335, Moorestown, NJ 08057, or call 609/235-0345. Although it might be difficult and somewhat expensive to make these in-house, you might like to see what can be done to give still transparencies animated motion. You are likely to see more and more of these on the instructional market in future years as individuals discover their effectiveness for certain subject areas. The cost of the kit is $3.50 prepaid.

6. If you cannot afford the expense of purchasing a dry mount press and still wish to lift and/or laminate pictures, then you should buy clear contact film and a roller to ink materials known as a brayer. Carefully cover the clay-coated picture with the film starting from the middle and moving out to the sides to avoid any bubbles. If any appear, puncture them with a small pin before burnishing the film onto the picture with the brayer. If you are merely laminating, you will not have to rub the picture as hard as you will for lifting.

7. For those fortunate to live in a large metroplex area, there are a number of photocopy dealerships that now provide color transparencies from computer-generated graphics. Since a large number of programs are available, such as Print Shop and Image Writer II, that will produce color IF the school or student has a color printer (ribbon), then this method should be tried to compare it with color lifting. Certainly, teachers and students will quickly recognize the lack of mess and the ease of making transparencies using the computer method.

One of the main reasons for using this technique is so that words and color pictures may be combined; something that is difficult to do using color lifts. For details on how to go about producing the camera-ready copy for the computer-generated transparency, review the contents of chapter 2 in this book.

TAPPING LOCAL RESOURCES

1. A professional photographer uses the dry mounting process in his or her work. A demonstration by this individual to show a particular technique for mounting photographs might be useful for students to see, especially if they are considering photography as a career option.

2. A local jobber would probably be willing to demonstrate how to make animated transparencies. Students might have their own ideas and a few designs ready in case the person has time to work with the group.

3. Invite a graphics artist to show how he or she designs the layout for transparencies to be used in instruction and/or business. Students should have questions ready to ask, such as, educational background of the artist; or time and costs associated with such work; other individuals the artist works with to produce the finished product.

4. The director of special education might be willing to demonstrate to the group how transparencies are being used with special students. Sample transparencies should be shown as well as a discussion of which students benefit most from their use.

5. An interested group of students might be encouraged to meet with primary teachers that would like puzzles and games laminated for repeated use by their youngsters. Samples of these items should be available for the students to show to the teachers to demonstrate that they are capable of handling such a project.

SOURCES OF EQUIPMENT AND SUPPLIES

The majority of the supplies may be purchased in your local discount stores. For laminating film, dry mount tissue, dry mount press, tacking irons, and mounting frames, you might want to write to one or all of the companies for a copy of their price lists for comparative purposes:

Seal Products Inc.
550 Spring Street
Naugatuck, CT 06670-9985
203/729-5201

The Highsmith Co., Inc.
P.O. Box 28005
Fort Atkinson, WI 53538-0800
800/558-2110

Franklin Distributing Corp.
P.O. Box 320
Denville, NJ 07834
201/267-2710

Brodart Co.
500 Arch Street
Williamsport, PA 17705
800/233-8467

The following companies handle overhead projectors:

3M Company
Audio-Visual Division
3M Center
Bldg. 225-3NE
St. Paul, MN 55144-1000
800/328-1371

Bell & Howell Company
Visual Communications Group
7100 McCormick Road
Chicago, IL 60645
312/673-3300

Elmo Manufacturing Corp.
70 New Hyde Park Road
New Hyde Park, NY 11040
516/775-3200

Charles Beseler Company
8 Fernwood Road
Warsaw, IN 46580
201/822-1000

Demco
Box 7488
Madison, WI 53707
800/356-1200

ANNOTATED BIBLIOGRAPHY

Barman, Charles. "Projector Care: Some Ways to Improve Your Overhead Projection Transparencies," *American Biology Teacher* 44 (March 1982): 191-92.
Author describes in depth a number of ways to make an overhead projection transparency more attractive, and gives directions on how to eliminate common problems of transparency display. Two diagrams are included.

Brown, James W., Richard B. Lewis, and Fred F. Harcleroad. *A V Instruction: Technology, Media, and Methods*. 6th ed. New York: McGraw-Hill, 1983.
The authors present how to use, mount, and store flat pictures. An entire chapter is devoted to a discussion of "transparencies for overhead projection." Illustrated.

Bumpass, Donald E. *Selected A V Recipes: Materials, Equipment Use and Maintenance.* Dubuque, Iowa: Kendal/Hunt, 1981.

Two sections in this publication deal with "Types of Transparencies" and "Mounting and Preserving Materials." Additional sections would benefit the teacher, such as puppetry and making movies without a camera.

Dardig, Jill C., and William L. Heward. "Back to Basics: Effective Use of the Overhead Projector," *Instructional Innovator* 26 (May 1981): 30-32.

Article provides instructions in the use of the overhead projector. It justifies the use of the medium in question, tells how to prepare transparencies, how to set up the room, and gives various techniques in enhancing the presentation.

DeChenne, James. "Effective Utilization of Overhead Projectors," *Media & Methods* 18 (January 1982): 6-7.

The author discusses the effective use of overhead projectors. Included are hints on how to select and prepare transparencies, and special techniques for using modes of the projector to make instruction more dramatic and useful.

Jones, J. Rhodri H. "Getting the Most Out of an Overhead Projector," *English Language Journal* (April 1978): 194-201.

The author examines the advantages of using an overhead projector, how to go about making a variety of different types of transparencies, and how to use both effectively in instruction.

Kemp, Jerrold E., and Deane K. Dayton. *Planning & Producing Instructional Media.* 5th ed. New York: Harper & Row, 1985.

Explicit details are provided (pp. 173-90) for making all types of transparencies, from the necessary skills required to completion. Illustrated.

Martin, Ron. "Telling Tales with Transparencies," *School Library Media Activities Monthly* 2 (November 1986): 40-44.

Using language arts as a backdrop, the author relates how he teaches students the techniques of producing hand-drawn and machine-made transparencies.

McCormack, Alan J. "A Method for Making Color-Lift Transparencies," *American Biology Teacher* 44 (January 1982): 40-41.

Article gives an easy-to-understand, upbeat explanation of how to make a color lift transparency. Six diagrams are included.

Media Production Series. Media Systems, Inc., 3637 East 7800 South, Salt Lake City, UT 84121, 801/943-7888.

In the series, the following would be of interest: "Heating, Laminating, Dry Mounting with Heat Press" and "Color Lift Transparencies." Either slides or filmstrips may be purchased.

Minor, Ed, and Harvey R. Frye. *Techniques for Producing Visual Instructional Media.* New York: McGraw-Hill, 1977.
The authors discuss mounting, laminating techniques, and producing transparencies for projection and display (pp. 159-99). This is probably the most detailed step-by-step procedure given in any production manual. Illustrated.

Mounting, Laminating and Texturing. Seal, 1986. (Available from Highsmith for $11.95.)
Seal has produced a comprehensive guide to the areas mentioned in the title of the publication. Although self-promoting of their products, it would be especially useful to reinforce the procedures discussed in this chapter and give the user ideas for additional activities.

Titus, B. "Lifting Transparencies," *Educational Resources & Techniques* 19 (Spring/Summer 1979): 29-32.
The author provides information on the materials needed and steps taken to produce transparencies from clay-coated pictures. Illustrated.

Wagner, Betty J., and E. Arthur Stunard. *Making and Using Inexpensive Classroom Media.* Palo Alto, Calif.: Education Today Co., 1976.
Authors devote an entire chapter to methods of "preserving" pictures. In addition to rubber cement mounting, they also describe hot-press mounting and laminating materials. In another chapter they discuss a variety of techniques for making transparencies. Illustrated.

Wittich, Walter S., and Charles F. Schuller. *Instructional Technology: Its Nature and Use.* 6th ed. New York: Harper & Row, 1979.
A discussion is given on the uses of transparencies and the equipment necessary for overhead projection. The authors also present information on the advantages and disadvantages of using flat pictures in the curriculum. Illustrated.

Yeamans, George T. *Transparency Making Made Easy.* Muncie, Ind.: Ball State University Bookstore, 1977.
A "self-instructional workbook ... programmed to provide initial instruction in a simplified manner to anyone interested in learning the basic procedures for making visuals for use on the overhead projector." Short, concise steps make this booklet ideal for the beginning student interested in making transparencies.

4

Slide/Tape and Filmstrip/Tape Presentations

INTRODUCTION

A note of caution before beginning to create a filmstrip or a slide tape presentation: Don't tell anyone that you are considering either presentation until you have made up your mind to do it. The main reason for this is that many individuals have tried these productions before, either by themselves or with a group, and have experienced numerous frustrations or have met with failure. Why? Very simply—lack of planning: "The cart was put before the horse!" This activity, like the others in this handbook, must be storyboarded *before* one begins to draw, photograph, or tape. Even with proper planning, you still must allot several hours per day—one hour for you and one for working with the group—over several weeks to complete the project.

Since much of what is covered in the area of photography is basic to both productions, the two presentations have been combined. Whenever there are unique features of one as compared to the other, these are clearly labeled slide or filmstrip production. Objectives and strategies for each are contained in the section dealing with the individual topics.

DEFINITION OF TERMS

35mm SLR Camera: A (S)ingle (L)ens (R)eflex camera which uses 35mm film and allows the viewer, when looking through the lens of the camera, to see exactly what will be recorded on the film.

Slide: 35mm film with one exposure each which has been mounted in a

cardboard or plastic frame for ease of handling and single viewing in a projector or hand viewer.

Filmstrip: A continuous roll of developed film with pictures on the film

correctly spaced so that, when placed in a filmstrip projector or viewer, they may be seen one at a time; since the film is 35mm, sprockets will be down both sides so that the finished product may be used in a projector or viewer.

Close-up rings: Extender rings which increase the focus power of your

camera so that it (the lens) will focus closer to the picture; this will allow the viewer to focus on the smallest of pictures; +1, +2, or +4 extender rings added to your lens will enable you to copy a picture down to 2x3 inches.

Copy stand: Equipment which is designed to hold the camera parallel and

above the pictures; when you use a copy stand and camera, you will want to have a cable release so as not to shake the camera when taking the pictures.

Cable release: An attachment which screws into the shutter release mechanism of the camera and keeps the photographer from jarring it when taking the picture.

Tripod: A three-pronged stand which allows you to mount the camera on top; a cable release should also be used with this once the pictures are framed and in focus.

Light box or slide sorter: A clear plastic box with a light behind it to view the slides individually and to place all of the slides of the presentation into proper sequence.

Slide projector: Equipment used to project each slide. A zoom lens with automatic focus and a remote control are two features which, when added to the projector, will make the showing of the finished program easier.

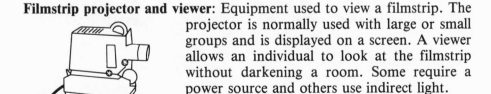

Filmstrip projector and viewer: Equipment used to view a filmstrip. The projector is normally used with large or small groups and is displayed on a screen. A viewer allows an individual to look at the filmstrip without darkening a room. Some require a power source and others use indirect light.

Cassette tape recorder: A tape recorder which will accept individual audio cassettes varying in recording time from 30-90 minutes; some units have built-in microphones; others have microphones that can be held or propped on a stand.

MATERIALS AND COSTS

The cost of materials will vary somewhat depending on your locale; however, by shopping wisely and comparing prices from at least three distributors for each item, you should be able to save money.

EQUIPMENT

Camera

Almost any 35mm SLR camera is suitable for copy work. I have a preference for certain brand names — Canon, Nikon, or Minolta; yet I have used numerous others for large group productions. Most cameras typically come with a standard f/1.7 or 1.8 50mm lens and built-in light meter and sell for around $200-$350.

Close-up rings

Also called extender rings or magnifying lenses, close-up rings will fluctuate in price depending upon the 35mm camera you purchase. For most cameras you can purchase an adapter which will allow you to use a variety of different makes. Each ring (+ 1, + 2, or + 4), which moves the focus of the larger lens closer to the picture, will cost around $6.50 each. Total cost purchased as a unit for all three lenses is approximately $20.

Copy stand

A copy stand that will serve your needs should not exceed $130. If you do comparative shopping with your camera in hand to check for placement of the camera on the stand, you will probably be able to find a durable stand for this price.

Cable release

A cable release should run no more than $6 and may be purchased from almost any dealer selling photographic equipment.

Tripod

Using comparative pricing and proper investigation, a tripod should not cost any more than $30. The same tripod can be used with a small video camera, so you are buying one item to serve several needs.

Light box or slide sorter

A variety of light boxes or slide sorters are on the market. Surprisingly, they are sometimes hard to locate unless you can accurately describe over the phone what you want or unless you have a picture of the exact model desired. Your camera or photographic dealer may have some suggestions on where to go for this item. For your purpose, you do not need the most expensive slide sorter on the market. A small unit will sell for around $25.

Slide projector

There are a variety of slide projectors on the market today. Bell & Howell and Kodak are perhaps two of the leaders in the field; either one should give you excellent service. Depending upon the features you desire, such as manual or remote control focusing, remote slide control, zoom lens, automatic slide change at 5-, 8-, or 15-second intervals, you should expect to pay between $300-$450.

Sound slide projectors with built-in screen

Panasonic, Kodak, Bell & Howell, and Ringmaster all have similar models of the sound slide projectors with built-in screens. If you are going to invest in this item, it is wise, if at all possible, to buy the model that will allow you the most flexibility. For example, most brands include the following: cassette recorder-player with pulse and stop-pulse capabilities (allows you to place an inaudible sound on the tape for changing slides automatically or for stopping the program completely); individual viewing of slides; headphone jack which allows for individual or group listening; and even more recently, zoom capabilities on slides for close-up viewing or for use of 110 slides which are much smaller than the 35mm format and thus require magnification. Some models will even allow you to project slides on a screen for large audience viewing.

Filmstrip projector and/or viewer

Dukane, Elmo, and Telex Communications are only three of the reputable leaders in the filmstrip projector field. A projector produced by one of these companies should not exceed $150 (without sound). A variety of combinations can be purchased in the projector/viewer line. If you decide to make such a purchase, I always advise buying the complete package so that you not only have projector/viewer but also a recorder/player all in one. The cost is not prohibitive if you consider that you have (1) a projector, (2) a viewer, (3) a recorder, and (4) a player. Current prices for this item range from $470-$550.

Cassette tape recorder

Beware. There is a wide variety of recorders on the market, some with an all-too-short life span. Buying a Sony, Panasonic, or Recordex (formerly Wollensak) should ensure that you have purchased quality and durability. You are going to pay more for any of these recorders, but in the long run you will not regret your purchase since it can be used for a variety of other productions. A reasonable price would be between $75-$150.

SUPPLIES

Cassette tapes

Most discount or drug stores carry cassette tapes. You not only pay for the recording time but also for the quality of the product. A 60-minute tape (each side is 30 minutes) should cost around $2.00 or less.

Film

Either 24 or 36 exposures of 35mm film may be purchased from discount stores or photographic dealers. Prices will vary very little among films.

Processing

Developing the film depending on the number of exposures (24-36) will range in price from $4.50-$6.00. The quality of the picture depends to a great extent on the processor, so choose one that you know is reliable for this quality.

SUMMARY LIST OF ESTIMATED COSTS

Equipment

Item	Estimated Cost
camera	$250.00
close-up rings	20.00
copy stand	150.00
tripod	30.00
cable release	6.00
cassette tape recorder	100.00
slide sorter	25.00
carousel slide projector	300.00
sound slide projector with built-in screen*	700.00
filmstrip projector	150.00
projector/viewer/recorder†	470.00

Supplies††

Item	Estimated Cost
cassette tapes	$2.00 each
film (24-36 exposures)	$5.50-7.50 each
processing	$4.50-6.00 each

*A sound slide projector with built-in screen is not essential if you have a cassette tape recorder and a slide projector.

†A projector/viewer/recorder is unnecessary if you have a cassette tape recorder and a filmstrip projector.

††Supply prices will vary greatly depending on your shopping ability and sometimes the area in which you live.

OPERATION CHECKLIST FOR THE
35mm SLR CAMERA

Manipulation of three basic adjustments on the 35mm camera will give you a perfect picture every time: shutter speed, lens opening, and focus. Shutter speed is controlled by moving the "shutter speed dial." Settings typically range from a full second to 1/1000 of a second or less. Moving this dial on the top of the camera, along with the lens opening known as the "aperture ring" in alignment with the meter needle seen through the "finder eyepiece," provides the correct exposure for the picture. Focusing the camera is done by looking through the finder eyepiece and rotating the "focusing grip" on the lens barrel until the picture is in sharp focus.

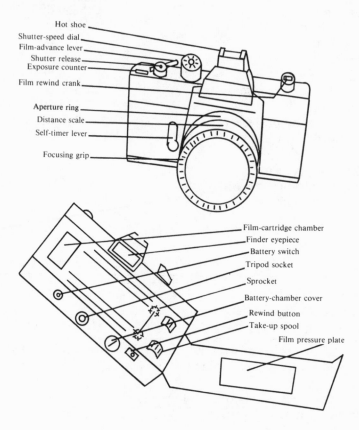

Hot shoe
Shutter-speed dial
Film-advance lever
Shutter release
Exposure counter
Film rewind crank

Aperture ring
Distance scale
Self-timer lever

Focusing grip

Film-cartridge chamber
Finder eyepiece
Battery switch
Tripod socket

Sprocket

Battery-chamber cover

Rewind button
Take-up spool

Film pressure plate

Checkpoints	Satisfactory	Unsatisfactory
1. Remove camera from case.	_____	_____
2. Remove lens cap.	_____	_____
3. Check battery power.	_____	_____
4. Turn battery *on*.	_____	_____
5. Open back cover and insert film.	_____	_____
6. Set film-speed window to correct ASA as shown on film box.	_____	_____
7. Check viewfinder for focus and exposure.	_____	_____
8. Set focus.	_____	_____
9. Set aperture ring according to meter indication (align needle and ring or consult manual).	_____	_____
10. Attach cable release and take picture.	_____	_____
11. Advance film for next picture (film advance lever).	_____	_____
12. Clip lens cap back onto lens.	_____	_____
13. Return camera to case.	_____	_____
Optional: Clean lens.		

OPERATION CHECKLIST FOR THE SLIDE PROJECTOR

Checkpoints	Satisfactory	Unsatisfactory
1. Locate the electrical plug underneath the projector.	_____	_____
2. Take the cord out of the casing and plug into outlet.	_____	_____
3. Insert lens in projector.	_____	_____
4. Turn ON switch to first lamp position.	_____	_____
5. Adjust levelers at front and side so that light is falling onto screen.	_____	_____
6. Position slide tray at zero setting.	_____	_____
7. Connect remote control and push FORWARD to advance to slide #1.	_____	_____
8. Adjust picture size by rotating lens with hand if zoom lens is being used.	_____	_____
9. Using focus knob, adjust for clearness of the image.	_____	_____
10. To remove slide tray, push SELECT bar and rotate tray to zero.	_____	_____
11. Turn projector lamp switch to fan and allow time for cooling.	_____	_____
12. Remove lens by pushing focus knob to the side, then pulling lens gently forward.	_____	_____
13. Turn machine off and unplug.	_____	_____
14. Return cord to case and store machine, lens, and slide tray.	_____	_____

OPERATION CHECKLIST FOR THE
FILMSTRIP PROJECTOR

Checkpoints	Satisfactory	Unsatisfactory
1. Remove the projector from the case.	_____	_____
2. Attach the electrical cord, and plug into wall.	_____	_____
3. Move ON-OFF switch slowly from OFF to FAN to ON.	_____	_____
4. Rotate lens barrel or knob until clear image is projected on screen.	_____	_____
5. Hold filmstrip in front of light source to make sure it is at beginning.	_____	_____
6. Turn filmstrip upside down and insert gently into gateway.	_____	_____
7. When film cannot be inserted further, revolve take-up spool until the filmstrip is caught on sprockets.	_____	_____
8. Using the framer mechanism, align a full frame before beginning the cassette tape.	_____	_____
9. Turn the ON-OFF switch to FAN until ready to show the filmstrip.	_____	_____
10. After showing the film, rewind it using fingertips to hold the sides.	_____	_____
11. Place filmstrip in container for storage.	_____	_____
12. When fan has cooled projector lamp, turn switch to OFF position.	_____	_____
13. Unplug projector and return to case.	_____	_____

OPERATION CHECKLIST FOR THE CASSETTE AUDIOTAPE RECORDER

Checkpoints	Satisfactory	Unsatisfactory
1. Connect power source. (If battery-operated, check strength of batteries.)	_____	_____
2. Insert cassette audiotape.	_____	_____
3. If using counter, reset to zero.	_____	_____
4. Make sure tape is on left reel. Push rewind, if not. If just operating, push PLAY button to start.	_____	_____
5. Connect microphone, if recording. If off-on switch is on microphone, switch to OFF.	_____	_____
6. Adjust volume/tone to middle range (some have an automatic volume setting).	_____	_____
7. Push RECORD/PLAY buttons.	_____	_____
8. Move OFF switch to ON on microphone.	_____	_____
9. Record a one-minute segment to test for proper volume level.	_____	_____
10. Rewind and play test recording. Readjust volume control if necessary.	_____	_____
11. Rewind test and push microphone switch to OFF. Push RECORD/PLAY buttons and record.	_____	_____
12. Rewind cassette and remove.	_____	_____
13. Unplug microphone and power cord.	_____	_____
14. Store accessories.	_____	_____

Note: Most tape recorders have a STOP button. This should be used to stop the machine *before* pushing other functions.

BASIC CONSIDERATIONS

ART WORK

The basic decision to be reached before any work begins is who will be responsible for the actual pictures to be photographed. Does the group wish to contribute individually or do they want an art committee responsible for all the pictures? There are advantages and disadvantages to either of the two choices. If the entire group contributes, each member will feel a real sense of accomplishment when they view their pictures on the screen, or they may feel a sense of embarrassment. If an art committee produces all of the pictures, the final production will probably be more consistent in form and look close to what it was meant to look like, yet this may cut down on the enthusiasm of the group. You need to know the desire and ability of your particular group of individuals.

FORMAT OF THE PICTURES

The entire group should also be involved in making the decision on the format of the pictures. You have at least two choices to make:

1. Will the pictures be copied from existing photographs, traced from magazines, or will they be originals?

2. What medium will be used: crayon, pencil, felt pens, water-colors, tempera, or another medium?

A factor which helps to determine the answer to both of these questions is the age of the group with which you are working. A kindergarten group might become highly frustrated if members decided to make original tempera paintings, or a senior high group might be insulted if required to cut and paste pictures from a magazine.

CONTENT OF THE PICTURES

The group needs to be cautioned regarding the content of the pictures to be projected. If too much is jammed into one picture, there is no way the viewer can possibly take in the total display. Also, the colors used in the pictures should offer contrast and not be so dark that a person standing in the foreground of a picture cannot be distinguished from the background. The video (visual) portion of your storyboard should be clear enough to help direct the art committee in the selection of proper content.

SIZE OF THE PICTURES

Individuals need adequate space on which to produce their visuals. No problem will be encountered as long as they keep their drawings horizontal. Standard typing or construction paper may be used as long as the artist is instructed to keep the drawing centered.

HELPFUL HINTS

If you are working with a young group, you will probably want to encourage them to work with magazine or coloring-book pictures. They may want to add color to their pictures with crayon, watercolor, or tempera. Intermediate students might try tracing pictures from other sources. Tracing paper may be bought or the inside sheet of a ditto thermal master may be used—at no expense to you. Once the student has traced the picture and has the desired colors marked on the drawing, it can easily be transferred to regular typing or construction paper with carbon paper or the ink sheet of a ditto master—again, at no additional expense.

As the drawings are completed, make sure you number them on the back according to the script you will be using for the narration and taping. Check off each drawing on a master script as you record the number; this will help you and the group see how the illustrations are proceeding and who has not completed their work.

FILM FOR THE 35mm CAMERA: CHOICE AND LOADING

Slides and filmstrips may be made using a variety of film: Kodachrome 25 or 64 or Ektachrome 100, 200, or 400. The numbers indicate the speed, or how fast the film reacts to light. The higher the number the faster the film; therefore, less light is needed when using high-speed film. If you are going to be working with a copy stand or a tripod inside using artificial light, then Ektachrome 100 or 200 film is best. However, if you are going to use a copy stand or tripod outside or are going to be taking shots of buildings and/or scenery using natural light, then you should use one of the Kodachrome films. Kodachrome 25 or 64 will give you good results for the copy stand or tripod if you are using natural light.

Once you have selected the film, make sure you notice the ISO (International Standards Organization) number on the side of the box. For example, the box will have one of the following markings:

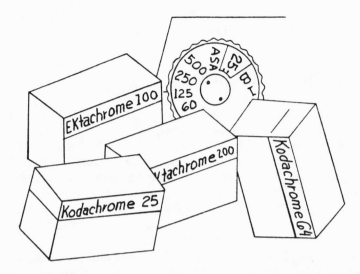

You will want to find the ASA dial (film-speed window) on your camera (refer to the picture of the 35mm camera on page 95) and pull up. Notice that the dial moves. Set the number on the dial to match the number on the box. You are now ready to load the film.

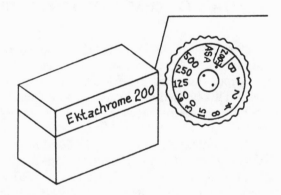

Loading the film in a 35mm camera is not that difficult. Once you have scanned the manual on your camera, you will be able to load the film very quickly. You do need to be careful that the film catches on the take-up spool before closing the back of the camera. This can be done by inserting the film onto the spool and then tripping the shutter release button (depress the button on top of the camera for taking each picture) until you can see that the film is winding around the take-up spool. Close the camera and check the exposure counter to see if it registers on number 1. I prefer to waste a few shots with the lens cover on the camera and the back open to see that the film is in place before the first exposure is actually taken. If you adopt this habit, be sure to advance the film about three frames after closing the camera back: this film has been exposed.

TAPING THE NARRATION

Once the filming is completed, you will want to practice taping the narration. One important point that needs to be mentioned is that additional time needs to be given for the viewer to focus on the visual. If you record straight through the script without pauses, you will find that once the slides are synchronized with the narration, it becomes extremely difficult to view the information, much less change from one frame to another and also listen to the spoken words. Practice taping the script and then combining the two: words with visuals. This will help you determine the total effectiveness of the presentation.

If you do not have the means to place an inaudible pulse on your tape once it is recorded, you will need to allow for an audible "ping" to indicate the change from one visual to another. This can be done by having a student stand next to the microphone while taping and, on cue from you or another individual following the narration, lightly tap a triangle or crystal glass.

SOURCES FOR EQUIPMENT AND SUPPLIES

Most school systems and public libraries have some arrangement with distributors of equipment for discounts below retail costs. If this is not the case, you will want to put the items out for bid after you have decided on particular equipment. This procedure should also be followed even if you personally want to buy the item—check a variety of stores and compare their prices before buying.

A good source to compare current prices is *The Equipment Directory of Audio-Visual, Computer and Video Products*, International Communications Industries, 3150 Spring Street, Fairfax, VA 22031-2499 (annual publication) for a listing of each item with specifications and price. Addresses for each equipment item are given at the end of the directory, if you should desire additional information.

Since cameras are not listed, you will need to contact your photographic stores for the particular SLR camera you decide to purchase, or write to the camera company addresses given in chapter 4, page 81. Most cameras will come with standard features—f/1.7-1.8 50mm lens, and built-in light meter. By talking with your local dealers, you will quickly learn their preferences for durability and reliability. You might also want to obtain recommendations on a copy stand and tripod that will meet your specific needs.

Camera companies you wish to contact for prices are:

Canon USA Inc.
One Canon Plaza
Lake Success, NY 11042
516/488-6700

Nikon Inc.
623 Stewart Avenue
Garden City, NY 11530
516/222-0200

Minolta Corporation
101 Williams Drive
Ramsey, NJ 07446
201/825-4000

Mamiya Division
Berkey Marketing Corporation
75 Holly Hill Lane
Greenwich, CT 06830
203/622-5000

Olympus Corporation
Crossways Park
Woodbury, NY 11797
516/364-3000

Konica Corporation
25-20 Brooklyn-Queens
   Expressway West
Woodside, NY 11377
800/221-9760

Pentax Corporation
35 Inverness Drive East
Englewood, CO 80112
303/799-8000

Light boxes or slide sorters are also not included in *The Equipment Directory*. If your camera shop or photographic supplier cannot give you the names of any dealers, you may want to write for information on their models and costs to:

Knox Manufacturing Company
Acculight Division
111 Spruce Street
Wood Dale, IL 60191
312/595-0300

Leedal, Inc.
1918 South Prarie Avenue
Chicago, IL 60616
312/842-6588

Bretford Manufacturing
9715 Soreng Avenue
Schiller Park, IL 60176
312/678-2545

Visual Horizons
180 Metro Park
Rochester, NY 14623
716/424-5300

Supplies such as 35mm film and cassette tape cartridges should be brand names: Kodak film and Maxell, Memorex, TDK, or 3M Scotch for cassette tapes. By buying brand names, which perhaps are a little more expensive, you will ensure the quality of the finished production and also the durability.

SLIDE/TAPE PRESENTATIONS—OVERVIEW

Within the "sample format and evaluation for making a slide/tape presentation" on page 87 in this chapter, the media specialist mentions as one of the weaknesses of the activity: "very time-consuming." However, I do not see this as a weakness if you take into account from the beginning that time must be spent for a quality production. If you find that you are taking 40 hours for such an activity, then something is wrong with the topic you have chosen to develop or with the organization of the procedures. Twelve to twenty hours should be long enough to identify a topic, write, storyboard and script, produce the art work, become familiar with the equipment, photograph the art, and tape the narration.

OBJECTIVES

To be able to develop a slide/tape presentation with or for a specified group, such as students, parents, or community.

To be able to synchronize an audiotape with the slides to produce a smooth presentation.

STRATEGIES

There are a wide variety of possibilities to interest a group in producing a slide/tape presentation. I have found that perhaps one of the best ways is to invite a parent to show slides taken on a trip and explain each slide. This is especially effective if you are studying the topic in class and the students are somewhat familiar with the subject matter. If the parent does not object, you should tape the presentation and, possibly, borrow the slides.

After the first presentation, have the students view the slides again and listen to the tape as a group activity. After each slide is explained, turn the tape recorder off and let the students condense the narration into one or two sentences. Have one student record the number of each slide and the suggested narration. When all slides have been viewed and a new narration written, ask the students to record their narration with an audible "ping" to indicate the change from one slide to another. Present your guest speaker with the cassette tape as a special "thank you" for his or her effort.

Another method that I have used is to buy commercial slides of my local area. I show these to students without narration; however, the students automatically respond with their own explanations of these familiar surroundings. The same procedure can then be used as with the guest slide presentation.

These are only two ways to get students thinking about their own slide/tape presentation. You may wish to use either or both of the above and then ask the group to suggest topics which they want to develop into a presentation. Also, you could ask students if they would be willing to show the presentation to other classes in the school and explain the steps they used to produce the finished product.

PROCEDURE FOR PRODUCTION

You are ready to begin working on slides if and only if you have completed the storyboard and scripting on a particular topic. Once you and the group are pleased with the flow of pictures and ideas roughly sketched on the storyboard cards and with the filming directions and narration of the script, you should introduce the following procedures for production of the slides.

THE 35mm CAMERA: COPY STAND OR TRIPOD

In working with slides, you have the option of shooting a variety of picture and/or subject sizes. Very simply this means that you can use the copy stand for taking the smaller pictures, then move the camera to the tripod for larger pictures or for photographing a subject, or you can hand-hold the camera for shots of individuals, groups, buildings, or scenes — all of which can easily be placed in sequence for the final presentation. For this reason, it is understandable why so many individuals prefer slide/tape presentations since this gives them the flexibility and freedom to rearrange or reshoot if one slide is not exactly what is needed.

If all of your slides for the topic you have storyboarded are to be original art by the students, you might consider masking each drawing for consistency and viewing. Using the dimensions shown below, produce a black mask made out of construction paper which you can lay over the finished picture on the copy stand:

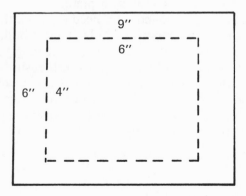

If students realize from the beginning that all of their work must be within this area, this feature will greatly enhance the quality of the finished presentation. Even if you desire to enlarge the drawings and move to a copy stand mask—multiply by two so you will have a mask 12x18 inches—you still will have the same slide format that will fit into the rest of your program.

CAMERA ON COPY STAND

When using a copy stand for taking slides, you do not have to worry about the direction of the picture or whether you are taking it upside down or right side up. Once the slides are processed, you have complete control over the way you wish the scene to be viewed or the direction a word will be read.

If a mask is not used to cover the pictures you are copying, place a black piece of construction paper on the base of the copy stand, and roll tape underneath the paper to hold it steady so it will not move as you position the pictures.

Place the camera on the screw mount of the copy stand and adjust the bracket until the picture can be viewed through the lens and brought into proper focus. If you have kept the pictures within the 4x6-inch format, you should experience no difficulty with focusing and framing the masked or unmasked picture. If the picture is masked, you might want to allow a slight margin of the mask to show on all the slides; however, if not masked, you might wish to lightly mark the edges of the placement of your first picture so that the remaining pictures can quickly be located on the same space. A slight margin is also advisable here so that you have a type of frame around the drawing to be photographed.

Once your picture is focused and framed, you will need to adjust the lights of the copy stand so that there are no "hot spots" on the picture. The light shining from the spotlights should be evenly distributed so that when you look through the lens of the camera, parts of the picture are *not* lighter than other parts or are not completely washed out by the bright lights. Be careful to check this with each picture.

When the lights are positioned, you need to check the light meter on your camera. Most cameras purchased today have a built-in meter which registers the correct amount of light. Again, knowing your camera and how your particular meter works in advance will ensure the best results. For most cameras, when you look through the lens you will see a needle to the right of the frame which will move if you place your hand in front of the camera. You will need to match up the circle over the top of the needle in order to have a correct exposure.

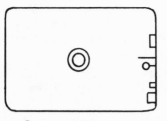

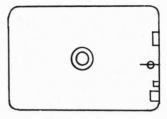

| Incorrect exposure | Correct exposure |

If you experience difficulty with this step, you should check with your camera dealer to see if your meter is registering correctly or if the battery which supplies the energy for the meter to operate is low or not working.

When the circle and needle are in correct alignment, you are ready to take your slides. Remember that if for some reason you move the camera while taking a picture or if you are unsure of the focus, you can always take another picture after you have repositioned or readjusted the camera. For best results when using a camera mounted on a copy stand, you will want to use a cable release. This keeps you from jarring the camera after it is set for the shot.

Cable release attached to 35mm camera

CAMERA ON A TRIPOD

The same procedure can be used with a tripod as with the copy stand. The only major difference is mounting the pictures. If you use the 12x18-inch mask, you will want to take it to a blackboard or staple it to a bulletin board and leave the top open to slide the pictures into place. If you use a black or gray piece of construction paper as a background, again you will want to stabilize it so that the pictures can be taped or pinned to the background. You have a wider range of possibilities to include in your pictures by using a tripod. So long as you do not go any smaller than 6x9 inches — the same size as the copy stand format — you can use your tripod to move in closer or move as far away as necessary. Suggestion: When making a slide presentation, if possible, take two exposures of each print so that you will have a duplicate of each picture (one for an archival copy and one that circulates).

PLACEMENT OF SLIDES IN THE PROJECTOR

Most individuals forget that a projector reverses the slide image. Very simply, this means that slides in your production must be placed upside down and backward in order to be viewed correctly. To ensure that you have them correctly placed, it is a good idea while your slides are still on the light box — in proper sequence and exactly as you would expect them to appear on the screen — that you use a permanent felt ink pen to mark the lower left-hand corner with a small dot. The slides may then be placed into the slide tray. Always check placement of these slides by projecting them onto a screen before the showing. A number on each slide may be useful also in case they are accidently dropped from the tray and have to be quickly replaced in sequence.

THE SHOWING

If at all possible, share the slide/tape FIRST with the group that produced it. Expect quite a bit of noise when they see and hear the presentation. Much effort has gone into the work, and they will want to enjoy their masterpiece.

MAKING A COPY OF THE TAPE AND SLIDES

This is the easiest part. Simply use another cassette tape recorder with a microphone or use a special direct hookup known as a patch cord. From the original tape use "auxiliary out" to "auxiliary in" on the other tape recorder. You will have close to the same quality tape as the original. (See illustration on following page.)

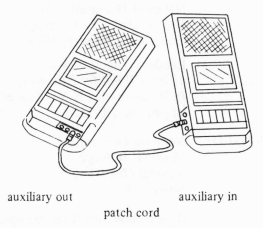

auxiliary out   auxiliary in

patch cord

Copying the slides of the presentation is usually much easier than copying a filmstrip. Most photographic stores supply this service at a cost of between $0.50-$0.75 per slide. Again, if you realize in the beginning that you want a duplicate copy of the presentation, it is less expensive to make the second slide at the same time you are shooting the originals.

SAMPLE FORMAT AND EVALUATION FOR MAKING A SLIDE/TAPE PRESENTATION

The following slide/tape presentation was developed by a high school media specialist working with a group of students in a special area— environmental science. Notice that the class was divided into three groups, which allowed each person to contribute in part to the total production. Documentation of the group, the specific objective, references, procedure, strengths/weaknesses, and the actual script are most helpful to have on file for future reference in case you want to share your experience with others who wish to see at a glance what is involved.

ENVIRONMENTAL AWARENESS

GROUP: Twenty-five students in an environmental science class.

OBJECTIVE: To determine and examine causes for the decline in the environmental quality of the earth and the progress being made in improving it.

REFERENCES: National Geographic Society, ed. *Wilderness U.S.A.* 3rd ed. Washington, DC: National Geographic Society, 1975.

Reader's Digest Association, Inc. *Our Magnificent Wildlife: How to Enjoy and Preserve It.* Pleasantville, N.Y.: Reader's Digest Association, Inc., 1975.

PERIODICALS USED: *National Geographic*
National Wildlife
Natural History
Newsweek

PROCEDURE: Divide class into three groups:
Group I: responsible for research, outlining, and script writing

Group II: responsible for selecting pictures and photographing

Group III: responsible for production (putting the program together, synchronizing slide/sound presentation)

STRENGTHS:
1. Eager participation by all; afforded the opportunity for all students to participate in some successful manner.

2. Provided opportunity for extensive research in books and local environmental conditions.

3. Developed environmental awareness on a local and personal level.

4. Afforded students an opportunity to use and become skillful in a variety of media and equipment.

WEAKNESSES:
1. Selected too broad a subject (one area might have been better, i.e., air pollution).

2. Very time-consuming; approximately twelve hours were needed from outset to conclusion. Some of this was used in becoming familiar with equipment. Group III found that synchronizing slide/sound to be frustrating at first.

SCRIPT:

ENVIRONMENTAL AWARENESS NARRATION

SLIDE #

1. Environment is more than a big word.

2. Our environment is a challenge to modern society and our beautiful earth is being eroded by many forces.

3. Our forefathers

4. found a land great in beauty and

5. bountiful in productivity.

6. As many pioneers exhausted their farmlands, they moved westward to more fertile fields, abandoning their poor lands to the ravages of nature. The abundance of land contributed to waste.

7. The population explosion and

8. man's technology have hastened the decline of our environment.

9. People (pause)

10. products (pause)

11. and technology are contributing factors to pollution.

12. Visual and noise pollution,

13. technological pollution,

14. careless removal of top soil,

15. strip mining,

16. acid runoff from coal mining,

17. soil erosion,

18. abuse of timberlands,

19. industrial dumps, and

20.   urban wastes are

21.   smothering humanity.

22.   Man is beginning to become aware of his environmental quality. He is taking steps to reclaim and protect his environment as in

23.   soil conservation,

24.   (pause: count of 5—advance to next slide)

25.   nature pathways,

26.   use of solar energy,

27.   energy conservation,

28.   even returnable bottles in an effort to

29.   restore beauty and

30.   bounty

31.   to our world.

—Eloise Reams

SUGGESTIONS FOR FOLLOW-UP ACTIVITIES

Refer to the same section in chapter 4, numbers 1-5. Some of the suggested activities for producing a filmstrip might be applied to the slide/tape presentation.

Additional activities you might wish to consider are:

1.   Once you have your slides in exactly the right sequence, you might want to consider making the presentation into a filmstrip. For the best results, you must send the originals; however, make sure you have a copy of all the slides in case they are lost in transport. You should first write for general information to one of the following addresses:

Nerge Film Labs, Inc.
1117 Fourth Street West
Minneapolis, MN 55066
612/388-8721
(ask for "Filmstrips from
35mm Slide Series")

Stokes Slide Services
7000 Cameron Road
Box 14277
Austin, TX 78761
512/458-2201
(ask for "Price List")

After reading their brochures, make sure you follow the instructions exactly to save them and you time.

A copy or copies may be made for the library/media center or for wider distribution throughout your school district. If you produce a slide/ tape presentation which is most unusual or which you feel is outstanding for the curriculum, you might even consider sending a copy to a publisher of multimedia materials.

2. Now that you have mastered the 35mm camera, you should try using a Kodak Ektagraphic Visualmaker which comes with an instamatic camera. The cost is $300. Two sizes are available: 3x3 inches and 8x8 inches—which denotes the size of the area which can be copied. Younger and older individuals have no problem using this piece of equipment on their own.

Photographs taken on trips, old postcards stuck away in boxes, or pictures from magazines and newspapers that a person wants to use in a report may all be copied using the Visualmaker and made into slides as long as they are no larger than the area indicated above. If smaller, you may want to use colored construction paper for a frame to lay the picture on or to give variety to your visuals.

For additional information, write to Eastman Kodak Company, 343 State Street, Rochester, NY 14650.

3. Your students might want to try their hand at making their own slides; three simple methods may be used:

   a. Drawing or painting on clear transparency film or on non-photographic film. This may be obtained from your photographic dealer or ordered from a variety of sources, such as

      Seal Products Inc.
      550 Spring Street
      Naugatuck, CT 06770-9985

      3M Company, Audio Visual Division
      Building 255-3NE, 3M Center
      St. Paul, MN 55144-1000

      The Highsmith Company
      P.O. Box 800
      Fort Atkinson, WI 53538-0800.

Transparency marking pens, water-soluble colors, food coloring, or colored plastic adhesive cut in a variety of shapes may be used to achieve an endless variety of effects. (See the articles by Allrutz and Bonial referenced in the bibliography for additional guidelines.)

If you use transparency film, it will have to be cut with scissors or a paper cutter to the proper size for placing in a slide mount. If you use non-photographic 35mm film, you can mark off the areas for the students to work within and then cut each frame for mounting.

    b.   Lifting clay-coated pictures using clear contact paper or laminating film: (1) Place the adhesive side of the contact paper against the clay-coated picture (some magazines are clay-coated, for example, *National Geographic*) and burnish the top of the contact paper with a coin, smooth plastic spatula or brayer; rub the surface until a consistent bond between picture and contact paper is apparent; soak (10 minutes) the combination in warm, soapy water until the picture can be peeled off the back and all of the white, filmy residue wiped off with a cotton swab or cotton ball (the original picture, now translucent, should remain on the contact paper); allow time for drying, and either cover the former adhesive side with clear plastic spray or use a clear floor wax to paint the back of the picture. (2) If you are familiar with laminating film, you may want to have your students place the dull side of the film against the clay-coated picture; then, using a dry mount press set at around 300° F, a tacking iron set on HIGH, or regular iron *without* steam set on "cotton," sandwich the film placed on the picture between clean newsprint or butcher paper and heat the film until it adheres completely to the picture (after you have tried this a few times you will learn the length of time required for the film to adhere using each method); the same steps are then taken as explained when using the contact paper.

    c.   Scratching on unprocessed 35mm film or on clear transparency film coated with water-soluble paints, food coloring, or a variety of marking pens can produce most unusual effects; if unprocessed film is used, make sure you scratch with a stencil knife, single-edged razor blade, or other sharp object on the dull side of the film, being careful not to cut into it; to add contrast you can paint the scratched design with colored marking pens or food coloring; if clear film is used, either side may be painted but be sure to make the color cover consistent and heavy enough so that it can be scratched away from the surface.

If you decide to make your own slides, then you will need to purchase slide mounts—either plastic which can be reused or cardboard which when heated and sealed may not be reused—for between $2.75-$5.00 per 100. These are commonly known as "ready mounts."

TAPPING LOCAL RESOURCES

1. Once students are confident with using the 35mm camera, invite a photographic dealer to speak to the group about the variety of cameras available for sale, the capabilities of these cameras and a few selected lenses.

2. Students might wish to take their production(s) on tour to other schools or public libraries. They should be prepared to explain the process and share any problems encountered while producing the program.

3. Your local historical society might appreciate a group of students contacting the organization and volunteering to produce a slide/ tape program for their permanent collection. Such a contact would allow the group to learn more about the community and serve the specific needs of an organization at the same time.

4. Many vocational/technical educators use the slide/tape format for their course work to provide introductions to materials difficult for a large body of students to see and for reinforcement and review before hands-on, individual examination of an item takes place. One of the instructors might be willing to share with the class some of these programs that are particularly useful, explaining specific reasons for their usefulness.

FILMSTRIP/TAPE PRESENTATIONS— OVERVIEW

Making a filmstrip for pleasure and/or for a particular reason, such as for placement in the school media center or for viewing by parents at a parent-teachers meeting, can be and should be tackled by any age group. The key to success is planning the entire sequence of events—from deciding on the topic to the actual presentation. If you organize the process FIRST, you still might experience some rough going along the way, but the likelihood of having a smoother transition from one stage to another is greatly increased.

I have seen some of the best filmstrips come out of a kindergarten class, simply because the teacher knew the level of the students and worked within it. On the other hand, I have seen a second-grade teacher almost in tears and students highly frustrated because the expectation level was set too high. For example, if after storyboarding your topic, you find that the students simply cannot draw the pictures they wish to represent the narration, then allow them to use magazine pictures which they have cut and arranged on the page, or let them use tracing paper to trace the pictures from a book. Perhaps an art teacher might shudder at this suggestion, but the purpose of all of these productions is to involve people in nonprint production—not turn them off! By all means, enjoy making filmstrips, and the pleasure you and your group receive from the experience will be evident in the final product.

OBJECTIVES

To learn the process involved and the equipment to be used in making a filmstrip.

To learn how to record the narration so that it is synchronized with each filmstrip frame.

STRATEGIES

My initial introduction in making filmstrips with a group came about as a result of a teacher's frustration in working with a low-ability group. She had tried every method possible to encourage her students to read. I suggested making a filmstrip which would require them to read from a number of printed sources found in the media center.

To motivate the group, check out a commercially produced filmstrip from the media center that has an accompanying cassette tape and show this to the class without explaining why. Once you have finished, ask them: "I wonder how difficult it would be to make a filmstrip of our own with a cassette tape, using a subject you want to develop?" Expect an explosion of enthusiastic responses from a captive audience. While you have them and before you select your idea for storyboarding, review the filmstrip/tape and have them comment on how the presentation was put together, the pictures, the narration, and any background music, etc. If they understand from the beginning that the task is not easy and cannot be accomplished overnight, then they should be able to settle down to the steps to achieve the finished product.

Once you have the finished filmstrip/tape and it is on file in your permanent collection, it can be used repeatedly to motivate others. More than likely you will not even have to advertise it — you will be approached by other interested groups who know by word of mouth that you have accomplished this feat; as a result, they can not wait until they have the opportunity to produce their own.

PROCEDURE FOR PRODUCTION

In producing a filmstrip/tape production, some of the same items need to be considered as in making a slide/tape presentation. The group needs to be reminded, however, that the format is different from the slide and that care should be taken to read this section completely *before* beginning.

PLACEMENT OF PICTURES FOR PHOTOGRAPHING

In case you have not realized it by now, every time you push the shutter release button on the camera you will actually be producing two frames for your filmstrip. Therefore, if you have a 24-exposure roll of film, you will have a capacity for a 48-frame filmstrip; a 36-exposure roll could yield a 72-frame filmstrip.

Standard filmstrip projectors that you use every day are made to project only a certain area of film. By photographing two pictures each time, you will produce a filmstrip that is on exactly the same format as a standard projector. Do not panic; it is really quite easy to make a filmstrip if you carefully follow the instructions on the following pages.

If your students have made their pictures 6x8 inches (3:4 ratio), you will want to use the format shown below with your camera mounted on a copy stand. Use a black or gray piece of construction paper measuring at least 12x16 inches. Find the exact center by measuring in 6 inches and 8 inches, and glue a small red circle at the center point. In pencil, draw two parallel lines 8 inches in length and 1 inch apart; measure out 6 inches more in both directions and draw two more parallel lines 8 inches in length. Label the first rectangle A and the second B. The bottom of all odd-numbered pictures will be placed on A, and the bottom of all even-numbered pictures will be placed on B. If your pictures are larger than 6x8 inches, for example, if they are 9x12 inches or 12x16 inches, use the same setup as mentioned above for approximately 1 inch between pictures. You will also need a larger piece of construction paper for background and your camera mounted on a tripod.

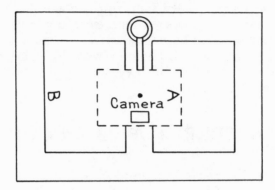

Camera Mounted on Copy Stand

Whether to use a copy stand or tripod with the 35mm SLR camera will depend on the size of your pictures. If the group has drawn their pictures 6x8 inches, you will want to use the copy stand; however, for anything smaller than 6x8 inches, you will need to invest in the close-up rings defined at the beginning of chapter 3. *Warning*: I would not advise having students work within a picture area any smaller than 6x8 inches, simply because anything smaller than this becomes tedious and difficult.

CAMERA ON COPY STAND

Mount the 35mm camera on the copy stand, making sure the light meter in the camera is working by turning on the two lights attached to the copy stand and moving your hand back and forth in front of the lens. This action should make the meter needle move.

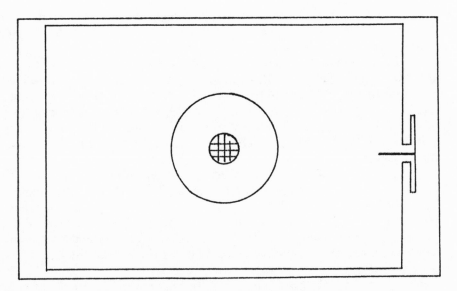

Needle on right indicates correct exposure.

By working with your camera, you should know when the meter indicates that you have adjusted your lens (f-stop) to allow for enough light to fall onto your film.

Place the black or gray construction paper background you made earlier on the base of the copy stand. When you look through the lens of your camera, the circle should be in the center, A on your right and B on your left. Allow for about the same margin around the outside of both pictures as the 1-inch space that separates them in the middle. You will have to move the arm of the copy stand up or down until you have this margin in alignment. Once you have done this, you should tape the edges of the construction paper down so that it will not move after you begin.

For best results, place the first two pictures under the camera, flat on the base of the copy stand. Focus the pictures and adjust the f-stop for correct exposure. Then place a piece of gray paper on top of the original pictures. Readjust the meter reading for the gray; this will allow for all of the tones between white and black to be taken into account and is actually a more accurate and true reading of the pictures you will be taking.

You will also want to position the lights on either side of the camera so that there is no glare or hot spot shining directly onto the pictures. Simply keep working with this until you are satisfied. Usually positioning the lights at 45 degree angles to the pictures is satisfactory. Remember that what you are seeing through the lens will be recorded on the film, so take your time.

To avoid camera movement when you begin filming your shots, you will want to attach the cable release to the shutter release button that you would normally push when taking a picture.

It is best to place the lens cover back on the camera, tripping the shutter with the cable release three times so that you have a six-frame lead to your filmstrip. Then remove the lens cover and insert the word "FOCUS" in large letters, for your first picture, and for your second picture "BEGIN TAPE." The third and fourth frames of your filmstrip will be the first odd-numbered picture and the second will be the first even-numbered picture.

Proceed slowly when filming. Check the order of the pictures and the placement each time before snapping the cable release. If you make a mistake—START OVER. This is the major reason for taking your time, since you cannot rearrange the sequence as you would if you were taking slides. When you have finished filming, reroll the film in the camera back into its container by pushing the rewind button release (on the bottom of most cameras).

Keep the drawings on file until you have received the processed film back from the dealer. *Be sure to inform the processor that this is a filmstrip; it must not be cut and mounted into slides.*

CAMERA ON TRIPOD

The same process can be used with the tripod; however, you will have to mount your construction background on a bulletin board or flannel board. Move the camera on the tripod closer or farther away until you have the center in focus and left-right margins in line. I have used straight pins to hold pictures in place, but I have also seen tape rolled behind the pictures, which is time-consuming but also gives a neater look to the finished production.

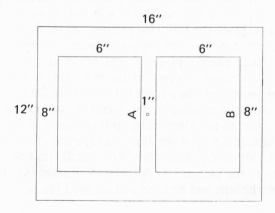

Camera Mounted on Tripod: Layout Arrangement

TAPING THE NARRATION

Time can be saved while the filmstrip is being developed by practicing the narration for taping. It is best to line the group up, with shoes removed and with a copy of what each is to say in sequence. If the class decides to use only two or three readers, then you can place them around the microphone in a semicircle for taping.

So that the individual operating the filmstrip projector will know when to turn each frame, it is best to record a "ping" at the end of the frame. The first "ping" should come at the beginning of the tape when the filmstrip is in FOCUS and thereafter until the viewing is completed. A glass or triangle may be used to create the "ping" sound. If you have more sophisticated equipment, you may want to pulse the tape with an inaudible signal after the recording is completed.

Stress the importance of not stopping after the tape has been started; if you do, you will hear a click in the tape each time you stop or start it. If you tape each practice run, you are bound to get one "take" that is good. This can easily be copied onto another cassette tape so that the best recording will be at the beginning of the program.

COPYING THE FILMSTRIP/TAPE PRESENTATION

Making a copy of the original filmstrip is not as easy as copying slides. For best results, you should write to the following addresses and request a price check on the copying of an original filmstrip. The price will range from $22.50 for one copy to $5.70 for multiple copies after the first:

Stokes Slide Services　　　　　　Nerge Film Labs, Inc.
7000 Cameron Road　　　　　　　1117 Fourth Street West
Box 14277　　　　　　　　　　　　Red Wing, MN 55066
Austin, TX 78761　　　　　　　　612/388-8721
512/458-2201

You may also want to ask your photographic dealer how much they would charge for the process. Also, if you know in advance that you want extra copies, it is much cheaper in the long run to make them at the same time you are shooting the original filmstrip, simply by repeating the process for each copy.

SAMPLE FORMAT AND EVALUATION FOR MAKING A FILMSTRIP

The following, "A School for Dolls" and "Adventures in the Forest," represent a report of an individual project completed by an elementary librarian for a graduate course in library science. Note the completeness of her report and the step-by-step procedure she used in working with the students in order to produce the final product.

Diary:
Making a Filmstrip

Steps

1. Discuss with a group of boys and girls about working on an original story project with magazine pictures as illustrations. The teachers and I decided to work with a group of third-graders.

2. Analyze structure of several easy books with children so that the students will have a guide.

3. Rough in a storyboard—story line and the general idea of a dialog in order to know what kind of pictures to look for as illustrations.

4. Select pictures.

5. Produce illustrations: cut, paste pictures, and decide on sequences using storyboard.

6. With pictures, write down dialog in detail.

7. Photograph illustrations.

8. Practice reading of script before making tape.

9. Make final tape.

Activity	Time	
	Boys	**Girls**
We discussed several books such as *Corduroy* by Don Freeman, *Whistle for Willie* by Ezra Jack Keats, and *Milton the Early Riser* by Robert Kraus. We noted the authors followed a three-step pattern. They presented a problem or situation which was then developed and finally resolved.	20 min.	20 min.
The boys and girls wanted to separate and work on different stories. The roughing out of a story line went smoothly, each group taking about 20 minutes or so. The draftings took about 20 to 40 minutes each.	20 min. 30-50 min.	20 min. 30-50 min.
When we came to the selection of pictures, we ran into trouble. It was difficult to find the pictures needed for their "plots." The children looked in stacks of magazines from beauty parlors and homes. The search took longer than we had anticipated.	3 hours	3 hours
The cutting, pasting, and printing presented no problems. As the children worked on the pictures, they also refined the dialogs.	2 hours	3 hours
The media specialist helped with photographing the pictures.	1½ hours	1½ hours
The practice reading and taping were made with a few more changes.	1 hour	1 hour
The final taping took longer than I had planned. By this time the children were quite particular about how they sounded.	½ hour	1 hour
	10½ hours	12 hours

Evaluation

Strengths

The Children:
1. were made more aware of the structure of stories;

2. had experience in group work and the writing of a simple dialog;

3. learned something of proportion and relationship of pictures;

4. practiced speaking distinctly; and

5. felt a sense of accomplishment and had a good time.

The Librarian:
6. learned about the use of a camera and the setup for making a filmstrip.

Weaknesses

1. The search for pictures was very time consuming. Perhaps we should have had more flexible story lines, but the children did not want to change their original plans too much.

2. Ignorance on my part of camera techniques. I was most fortunate to have the help of a production specialist.

SUGGESTIONS FOR FOLLOW-UP ACTIVITIES

1. Show the filmstrip/tape to another class. Have the students answer questions relating to the storyboarding and production procedures.

2. Send notices home via the students that a special showing will be held for all parents.

3. Let the students display the pictures used in the filmstrip, with the accompanying narration for each on a bulletin board.

4. Now that you have been successful with using a camera to photograph your pictures for a finished filmstrip, you should try another method perhaps as satisfying: drawing directly on 35mm film using pencils, transparency marking pens, or water-soluble colors.

If the media specialist has damaged filmstrips in the media center that can no longer be used because the leader has torn sprockets or the filmstrip has been ripped in half, trim away the damaged ends and bleach the film. Place the film in a mixture of one cup of bleach and a container of warm water until the strip is clear. Wash the film completely and allow to dry. Draw the following on a piece of heavy cardboard and cut along the dotted lines with a single-edged razor blade:

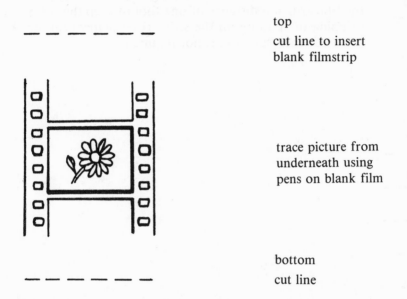

top

cut line to insert
blank filmstrip

trace picture from
underneath using
pens on blank film

bottom

cut line

Trace this and transfer on cardboard with carbon paper. Allow for a five-frame lead to the filmstrip. You may want to have students draw their presentation directly onto the film without making the individual blocks. If this is the case, you need to remind them that they cannot go beyond the area since this is all that will be projected. I prefer to draw the blocks for the entire filmstrip with a black marking pen, then tape the top and bottom leads to a table and draw the entire sequence without moving it. In the long run, this saves time since students tend to slide the film before the ink is dry, thus smearing the finished product. The filmstrip might look something like the illustration on page 104.

FOCUS

1ˢᵗ Grade
-Naming-

PERSON

STAR

FISH

☼

SUN

You should realize from looking at this filmstrip that not a great amount of detail can be included using this technique. The topic and the storyboard will have to be developed with this in mind.

To protect your finished filmstrip, you should use a clear plastic spray, such as Spraylon or Krylon, to ensure that the drawings will not be smeared. It is best to spray the film outside since the fumes are strong. Hold the can parallel to the filmstrip at a distance of one foot to keep the spray from dripping or spotting on the strip. If permanent ink markers are used, then spraying is not required.

Once you have used up the damaged filmstrips, your local photographic dealer should be willing to help you locate the cheapest means to buy 35mm *non*photographic film for this process. Buy in quantity if at all possible (a 200-foot roll sells for around $6.00). If he or she cannot locate a source, you may want to write to the following distributors for exact costs:

Christy's
135 North Victory Boulevard
Burbank, CA 91502
800/468-6891
(Ask for "Making Your Own
35mm Filmstrip: Instruction
Guide")

Prima Education Products
Irvington, NY 10533
914/591-8700
(Ask for "U" Film kit
information; cost: $29)

The Highsmith Co., Inc.
Box 800
Fort Atkinson, WI 53538-0800
800/233-8467

If you desire more explanation of this procedure, you might want to invest in "Creating Your Own Filmstrip," produced by the International Film Bureau, Inc., 332 South Michigan Avenue, Chicago, IL 60604; 312/427-4545. The kit contains a 50-frame filmstrip in color with cassette tapes ($59.00) and one box of twelve water-soluble oil colors, one number 3 brush, and thirteen 35mm blank filmstrips in cans. Additional paints, brushes, and 50, 100, or 1,000 foot lengths of film are available.

For those who do not own a camera, Creative AV Things, Inc., P.O. Box 582, Glen Rock, NJ 07452; 201/444-9525, for $8.95 will supply a mailer with predrawn filmstrip frames. Once completed in black and white, the artist simply mails the frames to this company, specifying either a 30-frame filmstrip or 12 slides be made from the art work.

TAPPING LOCAL RESOURCES

1. Contact an individual from the business community who utilizes filmstrips for in-service training of personnel. Invite the person to speak to your students on the benefits and reasons for using this medium over others. A sampling of these filmstrips should be shown to the students.

2. Students might want to contact the children's librarian at the public library to see if they could draw any of the picture book illustrations on write-on film. If this venture is successful, then the group might volunteer to write and illustrate some original stories for the librarian to share with her youngsters during story time.

3. A group of students might want to schedule an interview with a teacher or librarian to learn how filmstrips are used in instruction. They could also visit the media center to determine the variety of filmstrip titles in the collection and to see if deficiencies are evident that they could fill with their own productions.

4. If there is an audiovisual production specialist in your school system, he or she might be willing to demonstrate how to convert a slide set to a filmstrip. If students have produced a slide program that they want to donate to the library, this would be an excellent opportunity for them to learn how this can be accomplished.

ANNOTATED BIBLIOGRAPHY

SLIDE/TAPE PRESENTATIONS

Allurtz, Caroline C. "A Closer Look...." *Arts and Activities* 80 (October 1976): 44-45.
The author describes the making of light designs by students, using acetate 2x2-inch cardboard ready mounts, a slide projector, an electric iron, and common material, such as mylar, computer tape, industrial scraps, for visual display. Illustrated.

Barman, Charles R. "How to Prepare Clay-Lift and Sandwich Slides." *American Biology Teacher* 46 (February 1984): 120-21.
Article gives easy directions for making clay-lift and sandwich slides. Author claims the techniques are simple to master. Seven diagrams are included.

Barman, Charles R. "Using Transparency Film to Produce 35mm Slides." *American Biology Teacher* 47 (September 1985): 370.
Article gives directions on how to make 35mm slides using overhead projector transparency film. Three diagrams are included.

Bishop, Ann. *Planning and Producing Slide Programs*. Rochester, N.Y.: Kodak, 1984.
Written with a certain bias toward Kodak materials and equipment, this manual is essential for the serious student or teacher wishing to produce a quality slide production. The author discusses such information as planning, photography, preparing graphics, putting the show together, and postproduction.

Boniol, John D. "Making Slides without Cameras." *School Library Journal* 21 (April 1975): 36.
Three methods are explained in making slides without cameras: draw on/paint-slides; laminating film or contact paper slides; and scratch-on slides. Materials needed and helpful hints in producing the slides are also given.

Brown, James W., Richard B. Lewis, and Fred F. Harcleroad. *AV Instruction: Technology, Media, and Methods*. 6th ed. New York: McGraw-Hill, 1983.
Authors discuss informal and structured photography, production formats, presentation techniques, organizing a slide collection, and teaching with slides. Illustrated.

Close, E. Burt. *How to Create Super Slide Shows (for Fun and Profit)*. Cincinnati, Ohio: Writer's Digest Books, 1984.

The author provides a detailed accounting of how to go about creating a slide show from scratch or arranging slides already available. Short, concise chapters make the book quick reading and easy to understand. An added feature is how the producer (YOU) can go about marketing the finished product to publishers of nonprint materials.

"Creating Slide/Tape Programs." Sound filmstrip. Washington, D.C.: AECT, 1980.

The filmstrip with audiocassette describes the process of producing a slide/tape program. Ideas on scripting, photography, and audio production are covered.

Cyr, Don. "Making Color Slides without a Camera." *Arts and Activities* 74 (November 1973): 18-20.

The author shows how to lift clay-coated pictures for use in 2x2-inch slides. A materials list and ordering instructions are given. Given the date of the article, prices and addresses may be somewhat outdated and/or incorrect. Illustrated.

"Do It Yourself." *Media and Methods* 18 (January 1982): 22.

This article details the production of a slide show for instruction. Six steps, from the planning of content to the mounting of the slides, are presented.

Fraser, Duncan. *Photography*. London: Wayland, 1986.

A first book for those investigating photography, this would be an ideal guide for intermediate students. Minimal text with maximum illustrations make the book visually pleasing and informational. For those seeking background on the history of photography, the ten concise chapters are most useful.

Frith, Greg H. and Freddy Reynolds. "Slide Tape Shows: A Creative Activity for Gifted Students." *Teaching Exceptional Children* 15 (Spring 1983): 151-53.

This article discusses slide tape shows as an activity for gifted students. It goes into depth on the selecting of a suitable topic for the show, the writing of a script, the developing of graphics, the taking of pictures for slides, the developing of the audio portion of the show (including the use of music), the actual integration of the slides with the audio, and all budgetary considerations. The author claims the expense need not be great.

Garratt, Colin. *Taking Photographs.* Loughborough, England: Ladybird Press, 1980.

A step-by-step guide with illustrations which correspond to brief paragraphs as the author develops different points make this 53-page book ideal for the beginner. In nine chapters the author covers the basics of camera selection to photographic composition of pictures. Reference is given to other resources for advanced study.

Green, Lee. *Creative Slide/Tape Programs.* Littleton, Colo.: Libraries Unlimited, 1986.

A how-to guide over the sequential steps for successful production of a slide/tape program with ideas for K-12 students.

Jeffery, Lu. *Taking Photos.* London: Franklin Watts, 1982.

Although this is a British publication and some of the vocabulary might be strange for an American audience, it is comprehensive, concise, and should be understood by those wanting an introduction to the camera and ways to take photographs. The illustrations are particularly helpful and plentiful. Chapters are typically no larger than two-three pages. Of interest are sections devoted to making a darkroom, developing film, printing, and making a pinhole camera.

Kemp, Jerrold F., and Deane K. Dayton. *Planning & Producing Instructional Media.* 5th ed. New York: Harper & Row, 1985.

In one chapter, "Slide Series and Filmstrips," (pp. 196-212) the authors explain the process of taking pictures, processing film, editing slides, preparing slides for use, duplicating and filing slides, selecting a projector, techniques of projection, and use of the series. Illustrated.

Orgren, Carl F. "Production of Slide-Tape Programs." *Unabashed Librarian* 16 (Summer 1975): 25-28.

A detailed article which takes a step-by-step approach to the process involved in putting a slide/tape presentation together. Choice of medium, purpose, planning, technical considerations, and equipment needs are presented.

Petrone, Cheryl G. "Produce Your Own Slide-Tapes." *School Media Quarterly* 9 (Spring 1981): 206-209.

The process of locally producing five slide/tape programs on how to use reference materials in the school library is discussed.

Rebder, Denny. "The Final Countdown: Everything You Need to Produce a Slide Show In-house." *Currents* 11 (January 1985): 24-26.

Author details in depth the making of an in-house slide show and a plan to evaluate the forthcoming show's effectiveness. Article is more about the actual running of the show than the technical construction of it.

Reid, Robert K. "How to Produce a Sound/Slide Show." *Arts and Activities* 85 (March 1979): 50-51, 66.
The reasons for producing an in-house show, as well as the steps to follow for successful outcomes, are discussed.

Ryan, Mack. "Preparing a Slide-Tape Program: A Step-by-Step Approach: Part I/Part II." *Audiovisual Instruction* 20 (Sept. 1975/Nov. 1975): 36-38/36-38.
A two-part article which takes a step-by-step approach to explaining the details necessary to produce a quality slide/tape presentation. A number of helpful hints are given in organizing and selecting visuals and in the cost of basic equipment to film and tape the program.

Smith, Judson. "How to Use a 35mm Camera." *Instructional Innovator* 27 (April 1982): 14-15.
The author tells how one may use a 35mm camera. It describes an actual camera, its operation, its various lenses, and tells how light may be controlled to enhance one's photograph.

Turner, Philip M. *Handbook for School Media Personnel.* Littleton, Colo.: Libraries Unlimited, 1980.
Equipment and recommendations for taking slides are covered (pp. 61-66, 75).

Van Vliet, Lucille. "Flying High With Write-On Slides." *School Library Media Activities Monthly* 1 (March 1985): 40, 48.
The author focuses on production of a presentation using write-on slides. Step-by-step procedures are provided for replicating the technique with students of any age.

Wagner, Betty J., and E. Arthur Stunard. *Making and Using Inexpensive Classroom Media.* Palo Alto, Calif.: Education Today Co., 1975.
Suggestions (pp. 35-38) on how to purchase slides, add narration, and music are given. "Slide-making without a camera" and "cassette recordings" are also covered. Illustrated.

Wittich, Walter S., and Charles F. Schuller. *Instructional Technology: Its Nature and Use.* 6th ed. New York: Harper & Row, 1979.
Examines still projection, types, and equipment used. Briefly covers specialized slide applications (pp. 178-216).

Wittich, Walter S., & others. *Student Production Guide to Accompany Instructional Technology.* 5th ed. New York: Harper & Row, 1975.
The authors discuss (pp. 244-59) methods for structuring the presentation before taking pictures, use of the camera, single lens reflex cameras, slide formats, and organization of the processed slides.

FILMSTRIPS

Beatty, LaMond F. *Filmstrips*. Englewood Cliffs, N.J.: Educational Technology Publications, 1981.

Everything the reader ever wanted to know about filmstrips is contained in this concise text. The author traces the historical development of the filmstrip as well as its utilization, care, and future trends. A handy appendix describes how to go about splicing broken filmstrips for reuse.

Brown, James W., Richard B. Lewis, and Fred F. Harcleroad. *A V Instruction: Technology, Media, and Methods*. 5th ed. New York: McGraw-Hill, 1983.

Authors include a section on "uses of filmstrips by individuals" and also a section on "producing handmade filmstrips." Illustrations are given which display the process.

Cloke, William. "Filmstrips—How to Make Your Own." *California School Libraries* 47 (Winter 1976): 15-18.

In very simple language, the author explains "what you need to get started," "film," "lenses," "title and theme," "photocopy stand," "titles and inserts," "arrangement of slides," and "sound and narration." Illustrations of limited value.

Cyr, Don. " 'U' the Filmstrip-Maker." *Arts and Activities* 75 (April 1974): 40-42.

The author shows and explains how to go about making a filmstrip using "U" Film from Prima Education Products, Irvington-on-Hudson, N.Y. 10533. Illustrated.

"Filmstrips: Alive and Clicking." *EPIEgram* (April/May/June 1985): 14-15.

Author defends the utility of filmstrips in an age of computers and videodisks. The usual price of a filmstrip is given, and the author states that the use of filmstrips for instructional purposes is on the rise.

Kemp, Jerrold E., and Deane K. Dayton. *Planning & Producing Instructional Media*. 5th ed. New York: Harper & Row, 1985.

The authors devote part of a chapter along with slides to filmstrips: "format," "making a filmstrip from slides," "duplicating a filmstrip," "correlating a filmstrip with a soundtrack," and "preparing to use your filmstrip." Numerous helpful illustrations are given.

Ring, Arthur. *Planning and Producing Handmade Slides and Filmstrips for the Classroom.* Belmont, Calif.: David S. Lake Publishers, 1974. (Distributed by Fearon; available from Highsmith.)

The author offers step-by-step instructions and hints for the production of classroom teacher/student slides and/or filmstrips. Detailed examples are given for both processes.

Sunier, John. *Slide, Sound and Filmstrip Production.* London: Focal Press, Ltd., 1981.

Even though this is a British publication and some of the terms might appear to be different, this is a detailed explanation of the sequential steps in planning and producing both slide and filmstrip presentations. For the individual who wishes to go beyond the basics into multi-image productions, the last six chapters deal with this subject.

Turner, Philip M. *Handbook for School Media Personnel.* Littleton, Colo.: Libraries Unlimited, 1980.

Helpful hints and proper copying techniques are explained (pp. 66-70). Illustrations are simple and would be useful for the individual who needs additional basic knowledge before attempting the technique.

Wittich, Walter A., and Charles F. Schuller. *Instructional Technology; Its Nature and Use.* 6th ed. New York: Harper & Row, 1979.

Brief coverage (p. 186) is given to the advantages of students and teachers making a filmstrip for class use.

5

Single-Camera Television Programs

INTRODUCTION

No single medium has developed and changed more over the past five years than television and video systems. As prices for cameras and recorders have become more and more reasonable and as capabilities as well as ease of usage have improved, individuals in all areas of instruction have come to expect the medium to be an integral part of the school's equipment collection. Such expectation and wide acceptance makes its utilization easier for the media specialist to coordinate and integrate into the curriculum. Also, many homes contain such systems, so students as well as teachers are already familiar with their operation and use.

In *Making Television: A Video Production Guide for Teachers* (1981), John LeBaron makes the following valid point as to the value of the student's involvement in the entire process:

> Child-created video offers an excellent learning potential for students. Aided by good teachers equipped with video production facilities, children can interact effectively among themselves and with the outside world. Child-created video is an outreach through which the lives of children are meshed with the life of the local community of which they are members (p. xvi).

To say the least, students are ready to learn and experiment with this medium. If properly managed just like every other medium discussed in this book, they will amaze you and themselves with the finished product. This is a result of the increased sophistication and capability of the equipment in general.

Even as this introduction is being written the equipment continues to change; therefore, you, as the consumer, MUST consult with your local dealers, consider all aspects (YOUR needs), and purchase wisely with some vision for the future. For example, although much press has been given to the VHS-C compact versions of VHS first produced by JVC and the 8mm video cassette (about the size of an audio cassette) produced by Kodak and Sony, this is still not "the standard" for educational purposes and much fewer programs are available in this format. Therefore, it is better at this time to stay with what has become more widely used in this instructional circles: VHS—the ½-inch video cassette.

OBJECTIVE

To learn how to produce a video television program using the basic recording equipment: camera, video cassette recorder, and a monitor/receiver.

STRATEGIES

Introducing a group to this medium is like introducing them to an old friend. The only problem you will encounter is keeping them away from the equipment long enough for you to finish the demonstration.

It is perhaps best not to give too much advance warning that a class is going to be working with video equipment. If you do, this is all that will be discussed for weeks before you bring it into the classroom. Therefore, I have found that a natural "turn on" to use in introducing the medium to a group of students is to either have the equipment already set up in the classroom when they arrive or have the media specialist of the school bring it to the room as the class begins. Absolutely nothing has to be said on your part. Students will look first at the equipment and then at you until they realize what they are about to experience.

To ensure that the equipment is used properly, it is a good idea to show the group how each unit is attached to form the total system. If you have never had experience putting such a system together, you are bound to be fearful the first time. Ask the media specialist to demonstrate one time; then give it a try. If the media specialist is reluctant, read through the manual and do it on your own. You will be surprised how simple it is. As I so often explain to students, it is difficult to damage the system unless you drop it or unless you point the camera into direct sunlight. Reading the manual and carefully locating where the cords fit from the camera and the monitor/receiver into the VCR will ensure a system that operates correctly.

When you have interconnected the units and conducted some taping, let the students disconnect the system. As soon as they have finished, ask them to put it back together and begin taping for reinforcement. As long as you stay in the background, assisting when needed, the system should be easily utilized by your captivated group.

Once the students have had this brief encounter with taping at random, it is a good idea to show them a prerecorded instructional program and have them analyze (1) how they think the program was put together, (2) the different camera angles used, (3) the number of cameras used in the production, and (4) how many individuals were involved in making the program complete. Such an exercise helps to make them consider the time taken to produce a quality program.

Also, if you are going to take the time to explore the capabilities of television in the school setting with students, it is useful from an informational and motivational standpoint to visit a local television studio. Most stations are willing to schedule groups for a tour and a question-and-answer session.

If these strategies are used to interest the group in using the medium, you will have no problem stopping long enough to decide on a topic to research, develop, storyboard, and script for production.

DEFINITION OF TERMS

Single-camera television: Limited to the use of only one camera to visually record the program; all shots must be arranged so that one shot will smoothly lead into the next; most single-cameras should consist of a zoom lens, viewfinder, and tripod; some cameras, such as the camcorder, come equipped with a built-in microphone and small monitor for reviewing the taped program.

Zoom lens: Lens attached and in most cases built into the camera unit
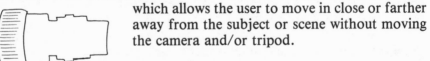
which allows the user to move in close or farther away from the subject or scene without moving the camera and/or tripod.

Viewfinder: Mounted on top of the camera for viewing the picture image; you will want to use the viewfinder to locate and clarify the subject you are taping before you begin your actual recording.

VCR: Stands for (V)ideo (C)assette (R)ecorder; similar to a tape recorder in that a cassette is used to record the audio and video, and the cassette is inserted within the machine for ease of operation; VCR units use either ½-inch or ¾-inch width recording tape; some of the most recent cassettes are even smaller, such as the 8mm cartridges.

Monitor/receiver: A television that enables you to watch the production as you tape to be certain you are recording what you are seeing through the camera; monitors/receivers may also serve as a receiver so that you can record and play programs on regular broadcast channels.

Videotape: Magnetic tape that has been specially designed to store both a picture and sound for playback; most units for classroom use are built to take ½-inch videocassette; depending upon the machine you purchase, videotape is typically stored on a cassette of 60-120 minutes in recording time.

VHS/Beta/VHS-C/8mm: Videotape formats relating to the width of the tape; VHS has become the standard size for instructional purposes; others are for home and recreational use.

Camcorder: A self-contained camera/recorder unit typically housing a camera for seeing the visual and an audio for hearing the sound; most allow for instant replay through the camera's viewfinder or through a standard television receiver; a variety of tape sizes located into the camera/recorder are available; most have or should have autofocus, zoom, manual override of the autofocus for filming outdoors, and rechargeable batteries.

MATERIALS AND COSTS

Video equipment is expensive—there is simply no way to avoid that fact; however, over the past five years, prices have continued to decrease with the advance of technology. A color video system will run, on the average, around $4,000 including the camera, monitor, and VCR. Because the color system is preferred by most buyers, equipment producers have, for the most part, discontinued reel-to-reel, black and white models.

Quality tapes from 3M, Scotch, Maxell, JVC, TDK, or Memorex, if available on state contract, might cost around $4 to $7 each for a 30 to 120 minute tape. If unavailable, you should expect to pay between $6 and $17 for the same tapes in record/video stores. Any one of these brands gives excellent color resolution.

SUMMARY LIST OF ESTIMATED COSTS

Equipment

Item	Estimated Cost
color system	
VCR	$1400
monitor (19-inch)	800
camcorder (camera)	2000

Supplies

Item	Estimated Cost
cassette tapes	$6 to $17

OPERATION CHECKLIST FOR
THE VIDEO SYSTEM

Checkpoints	Satisfactory	Unsatisfactory
1. Set up individual units:		
a. Place camera on tripod; plug into electrical outlet.	_____	_____
b. Place monitor on a cart; plug into outlet.	_____	_____
c. Place VCR on a cart; remove protective cover; plug into outlet.	_____	_____
2. Interconnect a, b, and c (cords are distinctive and may only be connected one way; refer to manual for unique features).	_____	_____

Checkpoints   **Satisfactory**   **Unsatisfactory**

3. Turn power switch to ON, all
   three units.   _____   _____

4. Insert videocassette into VCR;
   depress REWIND if using cassette to
   make sure tape is at the beginning.   _____   _____

5. Adjust camera focus, brightness,
   and contrast (some have a WHITE
   BALANCE that must be adjusted
   before you begin to tape).   _____   _____

6. Check monitor for picture
   alignment.   _____   _____

7. Push counter button on VCR to
   zero.   _____   _____

8. Depress RECORD/PLAY control
   and tape for two minutes.   _____   _____

9. Rewind tape to zero setting.   _____   _____

10. Evaluate contents by viewing on
    monitor.   _____   _____

11. Rewind tape and remove from
    VCR.   _____   _____

12. Turn power to OFF on all units
    and unplug.   _____   _____

13. Replace plastic cover on VCR.   _____   _____

14. Remove camera from tripod and
    store.   _____   _____

15. Return units to proper storage
    location.   _____   _____

PROCEDURE FOR PRODUCTION

The key to a successful single-camera television program is the advanced planning that goes into it before the camera and recorder are even turned on. I have witnessed too many frustrating first encounters by both teachers and students, simply because they felt that the finished product could be written, directed, and taped all in one meeting — IMPOSSIBLE.

As mentioned in the "Strategies" section, one of the best ways to turn a group on to the medium is with an initial introduction/demonstration/ discussion of its capabilities. After the initial introduction to the video system, the following steps might be taken in planning and producing the finished program.

1. Decide on a simple topic and develop the storyboard. You might want to be thinking about different positions for the camera, such as close-up, medium, or long shots, that will add variety for the viewer. Write these down under the picture as "special instructions."

2. Convert the storyboard to a script format. At this stage of development, you should consider adding an additional column not usually included in scripting — the camera column (check the "Sample Format" section for an example of this). The column is useful for the director of the program to check, at a glance, the sequence of events. Also, while scripting, it will help if you record an estimated time for each sequence under the video. More than likely this will change, but the group needs to know an estimated running time before the taping begins.

3. Choose the roles to be played. In addition to the actors, other very important people in the production are the camera person; the technicians who check the sound level, set up, and maintain the entire video system; the set manager who checks the placement of all the props; and the director who controls all the rehearsals and taping sessions. Some programs will require a narrator who introduces and periodically ties the production together. Also, depending upon the number and type of visuals to be used, a graphics committee may have to be formed. If visuals are used, keep the lettering large and the pictures as simple as possible.

4. Rehearse the program as much as possible before taping. Although with videotaping you have the capability of retaking the program until the group feels it is of acceptable quality, it is much better to work out the problem areas before the taping begins.

5. Try to arrange for an area or room for your rehearsals and final taping that is free of interruption from other classes and that is away from external noise. Most microphones used with the video system are sensitive and tend to pick up all extraneous noise. Constant interruptions by others or from an intercom greatly disturb the concentration of the group and the quality of the finished product.

6. If at all possible, try not to pause the tape. Most systems have a pause which will allow you to stop the tape without taking the machine out of the record mode. Unless your system is highly sophisticated, you will not be able to remove the blur that results from the pause. Therefore, keep your tape moving from start to finish.

7. For schools that have recently purchased a video system, in all likelihood you have a camcorder of the ½" VHS or 8mm variety as part of the total package. Students and teachers will enjoy the ease with which such a unit is learned and used. Carefully studying the manual is the key to success for maximum utilization since every camcorder is different and has unique features to achieve a variety of special effects.

    Many have a digital input keyboard which will allow titles and/or credits to be "typed" and recorded onto the tape. If this is the case, students should be encouraged to experiment first and then make this part of their storyboard and script for use with transitions from one scene to another.

    Another attractive feature that most units have available is portability; meaning that by using a rechargeable battery inserted into the unit, it can be taken anywhere for videotaping for a certain length of time. This feature allows students to produce programs when being separated from electrical power. Productions therefore will not have to be restricted to taping inside a classroom or library.

8. Most video recording/playback units have a pause control which will allow for taping or recording without producing terrible "glitches" or wavy lines when the tape is stopped and started again. This means that in planning the storyboard and script, a scene may actually be stopped from an indoor taping and moved outside to continue with little to no notice on the tape.

Another excellent way to use this control function on the VHS is to make this a planned feature of a program in which the viewer is requested to stop the tape for discussion/reaction or to move to another medium for additional instruction. Even with prerecorded programs, teachers might consider using this feature more often when points arise that need attention and/or discussion without the fear of ruining a tape while paused. Skipping over tedious matter while viewing a videotape is, of course, achieved with using the fast-forward also available on most recorder/players.

9. If you continue to use the video system in a classroom setting and your group is upper elementary or above, you might want to rent "The Electronic Rainbow: Television" (see entry in the bibliography) for viewing. This movie, although somewhat dated, is an excellent overview of all aspects of video.

SAMPLE FORMAT

Four high school seniors planned this instructional lesson on changing a flat tire. With the aid of their teacher, they developed the objective, grade level, range, prelesson, length, actual lesson, follow-up activity, and bibliography. In the script, a division for the camera was added with instructions for positions: close-up, medium, or long shots. Approximate running time for each section is recorded under the video in parentheses. The narrator speaks the audio throughout the program, even though the camera is not on him continuously.

LESSON PLAN

TITLE: PROCEDURE FOR CHANGING A FLAT TIRE

OBJECTIVE: To present safe and proper procedures for changing a flat tire.

AUDIENCE: Senior high through adult audience.

PRE-LESSON: The instructor might wish to relate how he or she had to change a tire and the difficulty experienced. Also, he or she might have the equipment necessary for changing a tire and review this with the audience.

LENGTH: Five minutes.

TITLE: PROCEDURE FOR CHANGING A FLAT TIRE

PURPOSE: This lesson will show certain safety precautions one should follow in the event of a flat tire. Also, the step-by-step procedure of changing the flat tire will be shown.

FOLLOW-UP: If possible, actually change a tire.

BIBLIOGRAPHY

Lane, A. R., and Pawlowski, J. G. *Tomorrow's Drivers*. New York: Harper & Row, 1965.

Ward, Roger, and Yates, Brock. *Guide to Good Driving*. Chicago: Lyons and Carnahan, Inc., 1967.

SCRIPT

Camera	Video	Audio
on title card	Procedure for Changing a Flat Tire (60 sec.)	
move slowly to Bill & then to car (long shot)	narrator (Bill) and car being driven behind Bill	If a tire should blow out or go flat, keep your head. Hold the steering wheel firmly, and don't allow it to be torn from your grasp. Remove your foot from the accelerator and concentrate on steering until the speed of the car has decreased to about 10-15 mph. Then begin braking gently, get out of the stream of traffic as quickly as possible, and stop in a safe place.
	(30 sec.)	

(Script continues on page 122.)

SCRIPT (cont'd)

Camera	Video	Audio
move to Tim and close-up of equipment	demonstrator (Tim) and equipment	Here we have a typical young driver involved with the task of changing a flat tire. The equipment used for most cars are a jack, broken into four parts (jack stand, jack level, jack handle, and the jack itself) and a spare tire.
	(10 sec.)	
follow Tim to ready the car (medium shot)	demonstrator (Tim) and car	In order to change a tire: (1) Set the parking brake and move the gear selector to PARK. On a standard transmission car, shift to REVERSE. If possible, block front or rear wheels. (2) Raise the hood and activate the emergency flashers or place some other warning device at an ample distance to the front and rear to warn drivers.
	(20 sec.)	
follow Tim to tire and jack (close-up)	demonstrator (Tim) and tire with jack	(3) With a screwdriver or the flat end of a jack handle, pry off the hubcap from the wheel. Loosen the wheel nuts slightly with the tire wrench. (4) Position the jack as the owner's manual indicates. Jack the wheel off the ground after making sure the

SCRIPT (cont'd)

Camera	Video	Audio
	(80 sec.)	jack stands straight and will not slip.
		Remove the wheel nuts and pull off the wheel. (5) Put on the spare tire and replace all the nuts by hand. With the wrench, tighten the two opposite nuts firmly to position the wheel correctly, then tighten the rest of the nuts with your hands. (pause)
	(40 sec.)	
follow to jack (close-up)	demonstrator (Tim) and jack	Lower the jack and tighten all the nuts securely with the wrench. Place the hubcap back on with a sharp blow of your hand, and put away your equipment and the damaged tire. As soon as you can, get the damaged tire repaired.
	(40 sec.)	
move to Bill (medium shot)	narrator (Bill)	Conclusion: Thank you. We hope this information will help you in an emergency when you need to change a tire.
	(10 sec.)	

SUGGESTIONS FOR FOLLOW-UP ACTIVITIES

Once the group has gained experience and a certain degree of confidence in their abilities to write, produce, and direct a single-camera program, members may want to tackle one or all of the suggested follow-up activities listed below:

1. Groups of all age levels enjoy acting out either ad-lib situations or events of an historical or contemporary significance. I have witnessed some excellent presentations such as when teachers have written down events in history that the students have been studying and asked them to act out the situations as they have understood them. When recorded on video, those participating in the presentation have the opportunity to replay and evaluate their production. If a mistake has been made, additional research on the topic and another taping might help to clear up the problem areas.

2. Using video for making a visual term paper is one option for students who feel restricted by the traditional written method. The same amount of time, sometimes more, is required of the student to construct a program that is both informational and visually accurate and appealing.

3. If a camcorder is available, students might want to research a local topic and do taping on location. Also, if a field trip is taken by the group, this is an excellent time to take the unit along and record different segments for discussion when the group returns to the classroom.

4. Current events of the school, such as athletic games, plays, and special speakers, may be taped for future viewing by groups wishing to learn from the resource.

5. Special experiments in chemistry, biology, or other science classes that might be too costly to repeat might be taped and played back in the media center for individual review.

6. Since most schools no longer have access to super 8mm movie cameras for producing animated movies, students might want to attempt an animation project using the Martino and Martin article, "Yes! Animation Is Possible with Your Videotape Recorder," see entry in the bibliography of this chapter. Success with this technique might be slow, but rewarding.

TAPPING LOCAL RESOURCES

1. Local television stations are most receptive to tours of their studios. Students will want to ask how programs are developed and finally taped. If possible, perhaps the group could observe an actual production being shot.

2. Most communities have access to advertising agencies that use television as their medium when working with large department stories to show a new item or to display sales. Students would benefit from hearing how the production agent in advertising goes about planning the sales campaign strategy, costs of advertising, career possibilities, etc.

3. For those students interested in career opportunities in broadcasting, a call to a nearby college, university, or local television studio might identify an individual who would be willing to speak to the group.

4. Students would benefit from observing any in-house instructional television capabilities of the school system/district. A tour of facilities, along with a demonstration by the professional staff with a showing of sample programs produced at the studio, would be appropriate.

5. Some of the coaches in your school might be willing to show how they use video in teaching specific athletic or gymnastic skills. If other concept videos are needed in this area, students might want to volunteer to develop these with the input of the athletic department staff.

6. Once students have gained confidence in their production abilities, they may want to offer a mini-course some evening for parents interested in improving their own techniques of videotaping at home.

7. A parent of one of your students might have developed a special interest and expertise in taking home videos. This individual could be invited to show the development of his or her productions over the years and address techniques that have changed as a result of experiences with the medium.

SOURCES FOR EQUIPMENT AND SUPPLIES

Since both the equipment and the supplies are expensive items, you will want to investigate the costs extensively before a purchase is made. A lease or rent agreement might be arranged to test the equipment in advance of purchasing. So that you have adequate background on what different brands of cameras, videocassette recorders, and monitor/ receivers have to offer, write to four of the leaders in the field for comparative pricing and specifications:

Sony AV Products
Educational Electronics Corp.
213 North Cedar Avenue
Inglewood, CA 90301
213/671-2636

JVC Company of America
41 Slater Drive
Elmwood Park, NJ 07407
201/794-3900

Panasonic Company
Audio-Video Systems Division
1 Panasonic Way
Secaucus, NJ 07094
201/348-7397

Hitachi Sales Corp.
  of America
401 West Artesia Boulevard
Compton, CA 90220
213/537-8383

If you request in your letter, they will send you the names of local dealers. These dealers should be willing to demonstrate their equipment and assist in writing bid specifications for purchase. For reference purposes criteria for equipment selection and definitions of terms regarding video systems are given in Kenyon C. Rosenberg and John J. Elsbree's *Dictionary of Library and Educational Technology*, third and enlarged edition, 1989.

Tapes for the VCR should be purchased from your local dealers; or, if a state contract is available in your district or system, then this will probably be the cheapest way to buy. You might want to write to these four companies for comparative pricing:

3M A/V Products Division
Building 223-55, 3M Center
St. Paul, MN 55144
612/733-1110

TDK Electronics
12 Harbor Park Drive
Port Washington, NY 11050
800/835-8273

Memtek Products
Memorex Audio & Video Tapes
P.O. Box 420
Santa Clara, CA 95052-0420
408/987-1000

JVC Company of America
41 Slater Drive
Elmwood Park, NJ 07407
201/794-3900

ANNOTATED BIBLIOGRAPHY

Adams, Dennis M. "Developing Critical Viewing Skills with Student Video Productions." *Educational Media International* 23 (June 1986): 81-84.
Article deals with the electronic media and how its impact on students can be carefully shaped by the teaching of skills of critical media viewing to students. Its main emphasis is that students will learn best how to critically evaluate the electronic media when taught how to produce videos themselves.

Brown, James W., Richard B. Lewis, and Fred F. Harcleroad. *A V Instruction: Technology, Media, and Methods*. 6th ed. New York: McGraw-Hill, 1983.
An entire chapter is devoted to television: viewing, use, type of equipment, and production tips on pages 264 through 289.

Casciero, Albert J., and Raymond G. Roney. *Audiovisual Technology Primer*. Englewood, Colo.: Libraries Unlimited, 1988.
A basic text, with chapters covering television systems, projection equipment and materials, and putting on productions.

Cheyney, Arnold B., and Rosemary L. Potter. *Video: A Handbook Showing the Use of the Television in the Elementary Classroom*. Stevensville, Mich.: Educational Service (P.O. Box 219/49127), 1980.
Written in a simple, direct format, this handbook would be ideal to use with young children to show them TV is meaningful in their everyday lives. Brief suggestions are given in the first chapter, such as identifying TV riddles, camera tricks, etc., to only name a few, to spark the child's interest. Additional chapters discuss ways to use television in listening and speaking activities, reading and writing, math and science, and social studies.

Driscoll, John P. *Communicating on Film*. Champaign, Ill.: Stipes Publishing, 1983.
For the serious and advanced student of either television or film production, the author provides the details for structuring effective communication using the motion picture medium.

The Electronic Rainbow: Television. 16mm, color, 23 min., 1977. Pyramid Films, Box 1048, Santa Monica, CA 90406.
Leonard Nimoy surveys the development of television, then discusses basic principles and mechanisms of broadcasting, and gives a brief overview of different kinds of TV systems.

Gothberg, Helen M. *Television and Video in Libraries and Schools.* Hamden, Conn.: Library Professional Publications/Shoe String Press, 1983.

Author discusses practical ways in which this medium might be used in library activities. Historical background as well as future possibilities are given. Details are provided on planning, programming, and production. The book contains a source books listing and a glossary of terms.

Hirschman, Robert, and Richard Procter. *How to Shoot Better Video: Especially for VHS, Beta, and 8mm Cameras.* Milwaukee, Wis.: Hal Leonard Publishing, 1985.

A basic techniques guide to video production, this manual would be useful for individuals with limited background on how to make the most of their camera skills to make quality, meaningful programs. Heavily illustrated throughout, the book would be especially appropriate for the visual learner.

Hughes, Karen, and Dan Smith. "Cheap Shots: Teachers Can Now Produce Their Own Instructional Videotapes." *Media & Methods* 19 (February 1983): 14-17.

This article deals with how teachers may easily make their own videotapes for instruction. It gives an extremely detailed description of the set-up of the camera and the production rig. Numerous figures and diagrams are included.

Kaplan, Don. *Video In the Classroom.* White Plains, N.Y.: Knowledge Industry, 1980.

As the author points out in his preface, the book "has been designed to help teachers initiate 'pupil-created' television in the school." Although slightly dated with some of the equipment presented, the techniques remain valid. Of particular interest to teachers are the exercises following each section which reinforce the details of each.

Klos, Thornton A. "Scriptwriting." *Educational Resources and Techniques* 18 (Spring/Summer 1978): 19-20, 22.

This article deals with scriptwriting for instructional television. The author details the importance of instructional television, gives the usual background and prerequisites for being an effective scriptwriter, and provides the scriptwriter's part in the process of producing this medium.

LeBaron, John. *Making Television: A Video Production Guide for Teachers.* New York: Teachers College Press, 1981.

Beginning with the basics and continuing with "beyond," this is the most comprehensive guide to video production using children and the school curriculum as the backdrop. In addition to a chapter on using video picture display, pre- and post-production techniques are discussed in detail. A glossary of terms unique to video plus a 15-page bibliography for further reference is also included.

Lezzi, Frank. *Understanding Television Production.* Englewood Cliffs, N.J.: Prentice-Hall, 1984.

For the advanced student interested in pursuing television production professionally, the author discusses the basic details as well as advanced techniques of studio production.

Macrae, Donald L., and others. *Television Production: An Introduction.* 2nd ed. New York: Methuen, 1981.

This is a basic guide to the technology of television and production tips. Written in an easy to understand language and illustrated throughout, this would be a welcome addition by the novice for reference.

Martino, Alfreda, and Ron Martin. "Yes! Animation Is Possible with Your Videotape Recorder." *School Library Media Activities Monthly* 3 (June 1987): 34-36.

The authors briefly discuss the advantages of using video over super 8mm to produce an animated film. Materials, storyboard, artwork, procedure, and audio dubbing are explained.

Mattingly, E. Grayson. *Expert Techniques for Home Video Production.* Blue Ridge Summit, Pa.: TAB Books Inc. (17214), 1983.

Although the title indicates the book is for the home market, the teacher and/or student would find it useful for quick reference. The author provides background as well as detailed information on the techniques of single-person television production.

McQuillin, Lon B. *The Video Production Guide.* Indianapolis, Ind.: Howard W. Sams & Co., 1983.

Everything anyone would want to know about the ins and outs of television video production is included from budgeting to people to horror stories. Intended for the serious, advanced student who wishes to pursue TV for a career.

Millerson, Gerald. *Video Camera Techniques.* London & Boston: Focal Press, 1983.

Devoted entirely to the ins and outs of proper utilization of the video camera, this is an excellent reference book for the serious student of television production.

Porter, Martin. *The Complete Guide to Making Home Video Movies.* New York: Simon & Schuster, 1984.

For the novice who wants to have a handy reference book available for buying and maintaining a video system in the home or at school, this is a perfect choice. In addition to covering all the basics one would expect – camera choice, camcorders, techniques, lighting, audio, planning, etc. – an informative 40-page buyer's guide and manufacturer's listing concludes the book.

Portnoy, Kenneth. "Video in Script Writing Projects." *Media and Methods* 22 (November/December 1985): 13-15.

This article details how students' standards of writing may be improved through scriptwriting for videocassette production.

Potter, Rosemary L. *Using Television in the Curriculum.* Bloomington, Ind.: Phi Delta Kappa Educational Foundation, 1984.

The author points out the problems as well as the potential of using television with young people. She then discusses major uses of TV in general and in specific curriculum areas.

Rapaczynski, Wanda, Dorothy G. Singer, and Jerome L. Singer. "Teaching Television: A Curriculum for Young Children." *Journal of Communication* 32 (Spring 1982): 46-55.

The author discusses a newly-devised curriculum to change the impact of television on young children by teaching them about it. The author gives the children six lessons; each one is described. The pre- and post-test given to evaluate the effect of the curriculum showed positive results of the program.

Satterthwaite, Les. *Television: Planning, Design, and Production.* Dubuque, Iowa: Kendall/Hunt Publishing, 1980.

Although somewhat dated in reference to equipment discussed, this is a basic guide for television production ranging from single camera to studio and multicamera systems to utilization. One of the most useful chapters deals with the production process from planning the message to the evaluation process.

Schorn, Jayne L., ed. *Video Magazine's Guide to Choosing and Using Your VCR.* New York: McGraw-Hill, 1986.

This is a one-stop shoppers' guide to the selection of a Beta or VHS video system. The editor surveys a guide to portable units, understanding the common as well as unique features, how to shop for the VCR, and questions typically asked. One of the most useful chapters covers care and maintenance of the units. A listing of video companies concludes the book.

Schroeppel, Tom. *The Bare Bones Camera Course for Film and Video.* 2nd ed. (16 Oviedo Avenue, Coral Gables, FL 33134). 1980.
A mixture of the basics of both the 35mm camera and the television camera, this brief guide is ideal for the beginning individual with little or *no* background with either medium. The author starts with how a camera works and continues with composition, screen direction, lighting, and concludes with the actual planning of the storyboard and script.

Sievers, Dennis. "Create Your Own Video Program." *Electronic Education* 5 (October 1985): 18.
Author describes the technical steps involved in making a videocassette program via a computer.

Smith, Welby A. *Video Fundamentals.* Englewood Cliffs, N.J.: Prentice-Hall, 1983.
The author begins with the procedure for choosing the VCR and then details how equipment works as well as use of sound, camera, lighting, and the production techniques and aids. He concludes with a glossary and resource listing.

Teneau, Richard. "How to Edit a One-Camera Video Show." *Instructional Innovator* 28 (January 1983): 40, 44.
This article tells how one may edit a one-camera video show. No details of equipment needed to edit a videocassette are included, but the article has many helpful hints on how to shoot the video effectively.

Utz, Peter. *Today's Video: Equipment, Set Up, and Production.* Englewood Cliffs, N.J.: Prentice-Hall, 1987.
This is the most current and complete handbook on video available. The author has included production techniques, purchasing recommendations, operation procedures, and guidelines for planning scripts, storyboards, directing, etc. A must for any library or classroom considering video. Illustrated.

Wurtzel, Alan. *Television Production.* 2nd ed. New York: McGraw-Hill, 1983.
This is an advanced television textbook containing 632 pages that would be perfect for the student who becomes interested in TV production and needs a book for reference and additional guidance.

Zettl, Herbert. *Television Production Handbook.* Belmont, Calif.: Wadsworth Publishing, 1984.
A 614-page textbook devoted to all the features of television production that a professional would have to know. Starting with the basics, the book quickly moves into highly technical areas with elaborate details for the advanced expert.

Sources of Additional Information

Association for Educational Communications and Technology (AECT). 1126 Sixteenth Street, NW, Washington, DC 20036, 202/466-4748.

The Association has a variety of print and nonprint publications about visual literacy materials and production of nonprint programs. Write to the organization for an annotated listing of their publications.

The Equipment Directory of Audio-Visual, Computer, and Video Products. International Communications Industries Association (3150 Spring Street, Fairfax, VA 22031-2399), annual. Also distributed by Libraries Unlimited.

Published annually for over 33 years, publication is a listing and description of hardware available from members and nonmembers of ICIA, the trade organization of the industry. The directory is designed to help buyers make cost-effective decisions on the purchase and use of equipment. No implication is made that the directory includes all equipment available. Endorsement is not implied, nor does omission imply lack of approval.

Audio Video Market Place: A Multimedia Guide. New York: Bowker, 1988- .

A compendium of nonprint information, *AVMP* is updated every year and includes complete information on audiovisual software and hardware. The reference section contains a calendar for nonprint events during the year; reference books and directories; periodicals and trade journals; national, regional, and state associations; funding sources; awards; festivals; and a glossary of terms.

Concannon, Tom. *Using Media for Creative Teaching*. Rowayton, Conn.: New Plays Books, 1979. Distributed by Independent Publisher's Group, 1 Pleasant Avenue, Port Washington, NY 11050, 516/ 944-9325.

The 76-page text is an illustrated guide containing information on equipment, film utilization, the overhead projector, storyboarding, videotape, and other audiovisual resources.

Dayton, Deane K. "Future Trends in the Production of Instructional Materials: 1981-2001." *Educational Communication and Technical Journal* 47 (Winter 1981): 231-49.

Author gives the predicted trends for the production of instructional materials until the turn of the 20th century. The results of a survey on the subject administered to instructional media specialists is reported.

Eastman Kodak Company, Consumer Services, Rochester, NY 14650, 800/424-2424.

The Eastman Kodak Company is continually revising and adding to their print and nonprint holdings for circulation and use by teachers and librarians. Costs for loan and/or purchase is typically inexpensive. Many items are free, such as *Montage*, a newsletter for educators showing students using and producing their own nonprint materials; *Teaching Tips from Teachers!*, a compilation of ideas sent in by teachers of their methods of using photography in the classroom; and *Visual Learning Materials*, a packet which is a sampling of selected materials by one of their photographic specialists.

Film & Video Finder. 3 vols., 1st ed. NICEM (A Division of Access Innovations, Inc., PO Box 40130, Albuquerque, NM 87196), 1987.

This edition replaces both the *NICEM Index to 16mm Educational Films* and *NICEM Index to Educational Videotapes*. In three volumes there is an introduction, subject index, directory of producers and distributors, and title sections. Another recent publication from Access is their *Audiocassette Finder: A Subject Guide to Literature Recorded on Audiocassette* (1986).

Kamenshine, Lesley. *A/V Troubleshooter: Audio-Visual Equipment Operation, Maintenance, and Repair*. Englewood Cliffs, N.J.: Prentice-Hall, 1985.

From lamps to laminators to visualmakers to dissolve units, this handbook provides basic information, such as operating tips, problem areas with causes and solutions for each, in-depth coverage of each piece of equipment, and a glossary at the close of each chapter. Every library or production center should own a copy of this essential guide.

Laybourne, Kit, and Pauline Cinciolo, eds. *Doing the Media: A Portfolio of Activities, Ideas and Resources.* New revised ed. New York: McGraw-Hill, 1979.

The editors maintain that *Doing the Media* is "intended to serve as both a practical text in media education courses and as a portfolio of ideas for the professional teacher, media specialist, librarian, and others engaged in formal or informal educational activities." The eighteen contributors show how nonprint may be integrated into both the elementary and secondary curriculum to make students aware of the influence mass media has on their daily lives. The book provides excellent details and step-by-step procedures for *doing* photography, film, video, sound, and other media. The seventh section deals with the process of designing "an integrated media arts curriculum." The final section of the book is an annotated resources listing of print and nonprint materials, periodicals, organizations, and media distributors.

Learning Things, Inc., 68A Broadway/PO Box 436, Arlington, MA 02174, 617/546-0093.

Write for a current copy of "Our Catalog." Materials and equipment for "Photography in the Classroom," "More Photo Stuff," and "Books" are available. Cameras begin at $6.50 each, with reduced costs for bulk orders. Expendable items, such as studio proof paper, chemicals for developing pictures, etc., are provided in small quantities for experimentation.

Leen, Nina. *Taking Pictures.* New York: Avon, 1980.

Using few words, the author of this book tells young photographers what they should and should not do when taking pictures. She shows the reader how to make a story with pictures and also how to create original backgrounds. In paperback.

Miller, Hannah. *Films in the Classroom: A Practical Guide.* Metuchen, N.J.: Scarecrow, 1979.

In addition to the coverage given to film in this guide, the author has also included a beginning chapter on nonprint media equipment, which covers such information as standards and maintenance of hardware and criteria for judging software selection. There are also six appendices that list details such as organizations helping teachers, students, and librarians to understand and use film, professional journals, free and inexpensive sources of films and distributors. The major portion of the text discusses such topics as "film techniques," "types of film," choosing, securing, showing, using, and making films for the classroom.

Minor, Edward. *Handbook for Preparing Visual Media*. 2nd ed. New York: McGraw-Hill, 1978.

The author discusses techniques for illustrating, mounting, and laminating materials, lettering and printing, coloring, and producing transparencies for projection and display. Each technique is explained in elaborate detail with specific line drawings accompanying the text for reinforcement.

Morse, Carmel L. *Audio Visual Primer: A Guide to Slide, Film, and Video Productions for the Novice*. Kettering, Ohio: Blackwoods Publications (PO Box 1831, Kettering, OH 45427), 1983.

As the subtitle indicates, this is a handy guide for the beginning student in the three media listed. *Brief* overviews are given for each as well as basic information regarding script writing, soundtrack, using volunteer help, hiring professionals, evaluating services, purchasing equipment, and legalities. A glossary concludes the handbook.

National Information Center for Educational Media (NICEM), PO Box 40130, Albuquerque, NM 87196, 800/421-8711.

NICEM, recently acquired and managed by Access Innovations, Inc., provides indexes to all types of educational media: 16mm films, filmstrips, overhead transparencies, audiotapes, videotapes, records, motion pictures cartridges, and slides. The publications are available and frequently updated in hardcopy or microfiche. The file (#45) is also accessible through the Dialog database information retrieval service for $70 per online connect hour. "NICEM is the world's largest computer-based system of audiovisual materials."

Oates, S. C. *Audiovisual Equipment Self-Instruction Manual*. 4th ed. Dubuque, Iowa: W. C. Brown, 1979.

This is one of the most comprehensive compilations of specific models of equipment by type on the market. The manual may be used for self-instruction or for reference when a problem develops during actual operation. Each unit is followed by a quiz to test the user's understanding of the printed text. Single black-and-white illustrations make the instructions easy to follow.

Petrie, Joyce. "Use Media to Motivate Gifted Students." *Instructional Innovator* (May 1984): 19-20.

This author tells how the teacher may use media to motivate gifted students in an honors reading program. The process from start to finish is outlined in eight steps, and helpful "do's" and "don'ts" are presented.

Rosenberg, Kenyon C., and John J. Elsbree. *Dictionary of Library and Educational Technology.* 3rd and enlarged ed. Englewood, Colo.: Libraries Unlimited, 1989.

Divided into three parts: criteria for selection of equipment, a dictionary of terms used in the field of technology, and a selective bibliography, this is a most comprehensive reference tool. Each piece of equipment is carefully analyzed citing exactly what should be considered in purchasing. Approximately 1,000 terms are defined.

Spirt, D. L. *Library/Media Manual.* New York: H. W. White, 1979.

As the author points out in her introduction, the manual "which provided instruction on how to get information from a wide variety of communication media, is for students ... who have had little or no instruction in the use of books and nonprint materials." The book is divided into chapters and subdivided into appropriate units, with a quiz following each chapter to test for recall. The first chapter is especially helpful, titled "The Library Media Center." In it, the author relates, "policies, resources, and organization" of a media center and "starting the research: using print and nonprint materials." Terminology to be used throughout the book is clearly defined. Chapter 2 deals with guides to use in accessing print and nonprint. Chapter 3 is devoted to specific reference books, and chapter 4 explains the research process: search strategy, taking notes, and formulating a mediagraphy.

Wein, Jeff. *The Big Picture: Photography and Slides in the Classroom.* Waitsfield, Vt.: Vermont Crossroads Press, 1977.

The book shows young children engaged in visual literacy exercises making their own slide stories. The why, where, and how of slide production are discussed in detail. Illustrated throughout.

"Your AV Programs from Kodak." Karol Media, 22 Riverview Drive, Wayne, NJ 07470-3191 or 201/628-9111.

Many of the Kodak sound slide shows or 16mm films that discuss photographic techniques and skills are now available for 3-day rental or purchase through this distributor. Write for a copy of their brochure.

Index

Animation
  television, 124
  transparencies, 60
Audio, definition, 2. *See also*
    Narration
Audiotape recorder, operation of, 76
Audiotape recording
  production, 80, 99
  supplies and equipment, 68, 70-71,
    81

Cameras for filmstrip production. *See*
    35mm SLR cameras
Cameras for slide production. *See*
    35mm SLR cameras
Cameras for video production. *See*
    Video cameras
Computer graphics
  community resources for, 33
  definition, 23
  example of, 27-29
  production, 26-27
  suggested topics for, 32-33
  supplies and equipment, 24
    sources, 29-31

Drawing on film, 59, 91-92, 102-5
Dry mount press, operation of, 42
Dry mounting
  production, 43-51
  supplies and equipment, 40-41

Film. *See also* Drawing on film
  laminating, 38-39, 41, 48, 52, 92
  35mm, 66, 70-71, 78-80, 81, 102-5
  transparency, 91-92
Filmstrip projector, operation of, 75
Filmstrips
  community resources for, 105
  definition, 66
  production, 95-99
  suggested topics for, 16
  supplies and equipment, 70-71
    sources, 80-81

Graphics. *See* Computer graphics

Lamination
  community resources for, 61
  definition, 38
  production, 48-50
  suggested topics for, 16
  supplies and equipment, 61-62
Laser printer, 23-24
Lifts. *See* Transparency lifts
Light box
  definition, 67
  source, 81

Narration, 80, 99. *See also* Scripting

Overhead projector, operation of, 43

Photography, 35mm, 83-86,
  95-98

Scripting
  community resources for, 16-17
  definition, 2
  examples of, 13-15
  production, 8-9
Slide sorter. *See* Light box
Slide/tape presentation
  community resources for, 93
  production, 83-87
  suggested topics for, 16
  supplies and equipment, 70-71
    sources, 80-81
Slide projector, operation of, 74
Slides. *See also* Drawing on film
  definition, 66
  projection of, 86
Storyboarding
  community resources for, 16-17
  definition, 2
  examples of, 10-13
  production, 5-8

Tape recording. *See* Audiotape
  recording

Television. *See* Videotape recording
35mm SLR cameras. *See also*
    Photography; Filmstrips;
    Slide/tape presentation; Slides
  accessories for, 68-69
  definition, 65
  operation of, 72-73
Transparencies. *See* Transparency lifts
Transparency lifts
  community resources for, 61
  definition, 37
  mounting, 39
  production, 51-56
  suggested topics for, 16
  supplies and equipment, 61-62

VCR
  definition, 115
  operation of, 116-17
Video, definition, 2
Video cameras, accessories for,
    114-15
Videotape recording
  community resources for, 125
  production, 118-20
  suggested topics for, 16
  supplies and equipment, 126